THE
NEW YORK TIMES
DAILY CROSSWORD
PUZZLES

TUESDAY

VOLUME 1

Edited by
Eugene T. Maleska

⟨ P9-BYB-161

IVY/TIMES BOOKS • NEW YORK

Ivy Books
Published by Ballantine Books
Copyright © 1997 by Random House, Inc.

ISBN 0-8041-1580-X

Text design and typography by Mark Frnka

Printed in Canada

First Edition: February 1997

10 9 8 7 6

Introduction

Welcome to the *New York Times Tuesday Crossword Book*. You will find herein one hundred puzzles, edited by the legendary Eugene T. Maleska, all of which originally appeared in the pages of *The New York Times* on Tuesdays.

The *Times* crosswords have traditionally increased in difficulty through the week, with Monday's puzzle meant to get your week started on a confident note, and Saturday's, worked on by most people at home, meant to provide a substantial mental workout. By introducing this new series of *Times* crosswords grouped by the day of the week, it is our hope that puzzlers of every skill will find the book that is just right for them.

This book of Tuesday crosswords, slightly more difficult than Monday's, rates about a "3" on the toughness scale, with Monday being a "1" and Saturday being a "10."

Your comments on any aspect of this book are most welcome. Send your comments, queries, or suggestions to me at: Times Crosswords, 201 E. 50th St., New York, NY 10022. If you'd like a reply, please enclose a self-addressed envelope (no stamp needed).

Best wishes for happy puzzling!

Stanley Newman
Managing Director,
Puzzles & Games

Published by Ivy Books:

THE NEW YORK TIMES DAILY CROSSWORD PUZZLES —
MONDAY

THE NEW YORK TIMES DAILY CROSSWORD PUZZLES —
TUESDAY

THE NEW YORK TIMES DAILY CROSSWORD PUZZLES —
WEDNESDAY

THE NEW YORK TIMES DAILY CROSSWORD PUZZLES —
THURSDAY

THE NEW YORK TIMES DAILY CROSSWORD PUZZLES —
FRIDAY

THE NEW YORK TIMES DAILY CROSSWORD PUZZLES —
SATURDAY

THE
NEW YORK TIMES
DAILY CROSSWORD
PUZZLES

TUESDAY

VOLUME 1

ACROSS

1 Gemstone
5 Rumba specialist
10 Inland sea
14 Take __ leave it
15 U.S. rocket
16 Strobile
17 Caisson load, for short
18 Valentino role
19 English art patron
20 Tad
22 Directive
24 Women's org.
25 Remotely
26 Directive
31 Insect stage
35 Zones
36 Sling
38 __ d'Orléans
39 Adorn, in a way
40 Intrinsically
41 Old Attic coin
42 Rochester-to-Syracuse dir.
43 Cantata singers
44 Suppose
45 Fitzgerald's Graham
47 Neolithic time
49 Refusals
51 Emulated Nurmi
52 Attributed
56 Secret

60 Singer Laine
61 Crop up
63 Arrow poison
64 Finale, for Furtwängler
65 French quisling
66 Watch part
67 __ off (irate)
68 Legal attachments
69 She: Fr.

DOWN

1 Thailand, once
2 Vapor: Comb. form
3 Frolic
4 Directive
5 Havana V.I.P.
6 Exclamation of disgust
7 Turns right
8 Loos or O'Day
9 Directive
10 Olivier and Gielgud
11 Appaloosa's relative
12 Against
13 Old manorial court
21 St. Louis bridge
23 Glazier's unit
26 Senate aides
27 March 17 marchers
28 Martinique volcano

2

29	Stimulate	46	Foray
30	Peter and a Wolfe	48	Bay windows
32	Shinbone	50	Caravansary
33	Get __ (move)	52	Pt. of C.P.A.
34	Biography by Freeman	53	__ gin
37	Gal Fri.	54	Yield
40	Directive	55	Jackknife, e.g.
41	Directive	57	Indigo source
43	Fronton word	58	True
44	__ even keel	59	Eliminate
		62	__ Vicente, El Salvador

ACROSS

1 Unskilled persons
5 Comic Wilson
9 Havana, e.g.
14 "L' __, c'est moi": Louis XIV
15 Sardinian coins
16 Worship
17 Provender
18 Austen novel
19 For rent
20 Snoopy's aerial adversary
23 "__ Kapital": Marx
24 Work unit
25 One-man boat
27 Pleasure-loving
31 Tape or wire joining
34 Former hockey All Star
35 Kind of owl
38 TV's __ Wences
39 Longest sentence
41 Understanding of
43 Exchange premium
44 Moves quickly
46 Textile workers
48 Purpose
49 Mexican dish
51 Football play
53 Arabian princes
55 He treats pets
56 Swindle
58 Peter Pan's adversary
64 Word of surrender
66 Pisa's river
67 "Winnie __ Pu": Lenard
68 "Merry Widow" composer
69 Ballet skirt
70 Monk's quarters
71 Prepare (fowl) for roasting
72 Receives socially
73 Daytime TV feature

DOWN

1 Adroit
2 The former Deseret, to an extent
3 Just sufficient
4 Kind of record
5 Reaching maturity
6 Branch
7 "__ La Douce"
8 Boscs
9 Herbal plants
10 Nuptials response
11 An 007 adversary
12 Sector
13 Softens by soaking
21 Kin of fulmars
22 Gives approval to
26 Kind of collar
27 Composer of "The Planets"
28 Writer Jong
29 Sax Rohmer arch villain

4

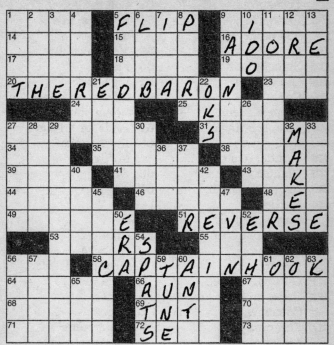

30	Firewood measure
32	Creates
33	Eat away
36	Minor street
37	North Sea feeder
40	Hard, yellow cheese
42	Prior
45	Kitchen gadgets
47	Swedish explorer Hedin

50	Distinctive time period
52	Rules of conduct
54	Petty quarrels
56	Ism
57	Rare person
59	Adjust exactly
60	Poker stake
61	Ersatz butter
62	Spanish cooking pot
63	Seaweed
65	__ Vegas

ACROSS

1 Transports
6 Chanel's nickname
10 Grouper
14 Slangily licit
15 Queued up
16 Cay
17 Contest scene
18 Steeple swinger
19 Italian coin
20 Grinder of a sort
22 Change
23 Laurel or Smith
24 Method of transmutation
26 Caledonian cap
29 Fleur-de-__
30 Bye-bye
31 Gift to influence
33 Came on like Casanova
37 Karenina or Christie
38 German novelist: 1837-98
40 Peace advocate
41 Mexican livestock-farm owner
43 Savory jelly
44 Metric measure, for short
45 Actor Chaney
47 Certain club member
48 Last at Belmont Park
51 Pelvic bones
53 Soft drinks
54 Returns, in a way
59 Mine access
60 Flex
61 Ingested
62 Dream, in Dijon
63 Commedia dell' __
64 Place for an élève
65 River to the North Sea
66 Org.
67 Alighieri

DOWN

1 Chopped cabbage
2 Olympus dweller
3 "__ a Kick . . ."
4 Aches
5 Shock
6 Staterooms
7 City on the Oka
8 Compiler
9 Screech or hoot follower
10 Foundry workers
11 Finest
12 Composer Ned
13 Eared seal
21 Has permission
22 Minutes of a meeting
25 Hoods' flights
26 Skier's lift
27 Writer Bontemps

6

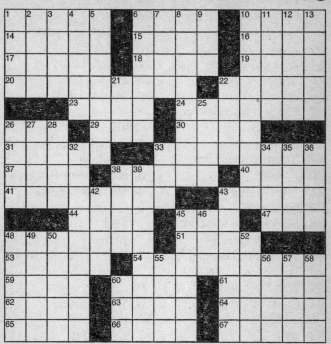

28 Gopher State: Abbr.
32 Retreat from a stand taken
33 Antique auto
34 Deal with trouble
35 Wicked
36 Array
38 Sniggler's prey
39 Arness and Graves, e.g.
42 Scurries
43 Fragrant ovule

45 Thespian Hal
46 Long in the tooth
48 Hair-raising
49 Mineral veins
50 Oil source
52 Manila hemp
55 Soldier and carpenter
56 Like __ of bricks
57 Prehistoric stone implement
58 Genu
60 Whiffenpoof cry

ACROSS

1 Push roughly
6 Catherine __, Henry VIII's sixth wife
10 Kind of sch.
14 Was concerned
15 Sector
16 Former divorce mill
17 Shaped like Humpty Dumpty
18 A Belgradian
19 Chemical compound
20 __ Aviv
21 Yellowish green
23 Former R.I. senator
24 Sign in the window of 51 Across
26 Type of lettuce
29 Bring up
30 What a tug does
31 Cash or cloth additive
33 Irritable
37 An original sinner
38 Gobi and Mojave
41 Tiller's tool
42 Actress Oberon
44 Morning moisture
45 Seeded
46 Woeful cry
49 Eavesdrops
51 See 24 Across
55 Hard to find
56 Reed or Hardy
57 Name
60 State confidently
61 Wahine's dance
62 Rebel
64 Spare
65 Egyptian symbol
66 Broché
67 Poet Sexton
68 Paving block
69 Minimum

DOWN

1 Carlyle was one
2 Possess
3 Evangelist Roberts
4 Experienced G.I.
5 Channel swimmer: 1926
6 Aisles
7 Van Gogh painted here
8 Primer, e.g.
9 Work havoc
10 Get ready
11 Extend a subscription
12 __ Gay, historic plane
13 Actress-singer Bergen
22 Causing goose pimples
24 Viewer-supported TV
25 Meal for Lady's Secret
26 Detail
27 Where vessels nestle

8

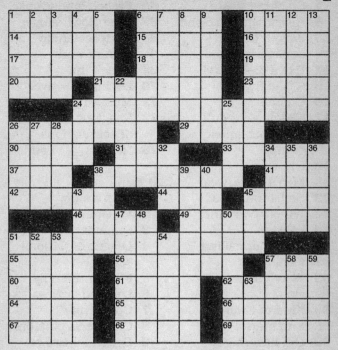

28 Jug
32 Carmine
34 Oxford
35 Hamlet grown up
36 Hankerings
38 Cancel
39 Germane
40 Strong cord
43 Penny Marshall
TV role
45 Swine's confines
47 Greetings in Oahu

48 Recognize rank
50 Hen tracks on
paper
51 Refrain words
52 Poe's one-word
bird
53 Of the planet Mars
54 Waistcoat
57 Callas was one
58 Employs
59 Proclivity
63 Caviar

ACROSS

1 Smelting waste
5 Apartments in Soho
10 Sacred bull of ancient Egypt
14 Use a dish towel
15 __ the Riveter
16 Custom
17 Middle East gulf
18 Chamber-music group
19 Ore vein
20 Men's underwear
23 Be left on base
24 Winery container
25 Laic
27 Career or calling
32 Facility
33 Wood for bats or skis
34 Kind of chair
36 Summarize
39 Gin flavoring
41 Decorated again
43 Hornswoggle
44 Cities' little sisters
46 Strength
48 Draw even with
49 Does a garden job
51 Avenger's action
53 Linen storage places
56 Chinese author __ Yutang
57 U.S. sports org.
58 Front-runners
64 Small Thames boat
66 French landscapist
67 Dust Bowl refugee
68 Early Icelandic literary work
69 "Mack the __"
70 Leningrad's river
71 Musical pause
72 Religious denominations
73 "Martin __": London

DOWN

1 Ship's mop
2 Venetian resort
3 Summit
4 League of Nations seat
5 More unfriendly
6 Lomond or Ness
7 Concerning
8 Children's pinafores
9 Bench for two or three
10 Shoemaker's tool
11 Women's short hair styles
12 Asian sub-continent
13 Beef source
21 False hairpieces
22 Identifying mark
26 Second-hand
27 Enormous
28 The former Christiania

10

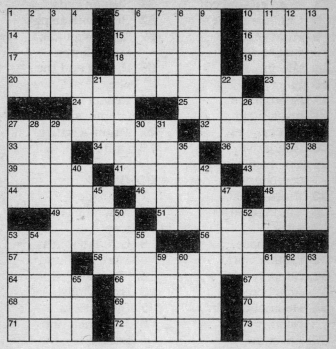

29 Gluttons: Slang
30 Canzoni
31 Lowest point
35 Casey and Mudville mates
37 Western Samoan capital
38 Strip bark from
40 A son of Seth
42 Gradually uses up resources
45 Percolate

47 Court order
50 Arranges in piles
52 Chant
53 Bank heist, e.g.
54 Summa cum __
55 Flat, round cake
59 Viking explorer
60 Easily swayed
61 Made do, with "out"
62 Tear apart
63 Actor Connery
65 Make lace

ACROSS

1 __ an egg (failed)
5 Chills and fever
9 Patio gear
13 Cay or ait
14 Disembarks
16 Sit
17 Bootblack's investment
19 "Jacta __ est"
20 Eucharist plate
21 Chemical compounds
23 Uninhibited
25 Kind of hanger
27 Fin
28 Fast; loose
30 Calif.'s motto
32 Slippery one
33 Acts bored
35 Homophone for wood
38 A combo
40 Something to read
42 __ on words (pun)
43 Impudent
45 Impulse
47 Uno, due, __
48 Afro, for one
50 Blackmails
52 What the blank in 19 Across means
54 "Home, Sweet Home" author
56 Helps
57 Ruins
59 Nautical call
61 Sick as __
62 Butcher's display
67 "__ is real! . . .": Longfellow
68 Epsom and the like
69 Redact
70 Umpire's call
71 Tatum's father
72 Optimistic

DOWN

1 Fleur-de-__
2 Kind of can or tray
3 U.N. labor arm
4 More profound
5 "Thanks __!"
6 High winds
7 By accident
8 McMahon and Sullivan
9 Petty fuss
10 Reached Olympic heights
11 River to the Rhone
12 Hector
15 Use scissors
18 Word with hose
22 Eject
23 La Scala offering
24 Disposed of quickly
26 Stratagems
28 Cliques

12

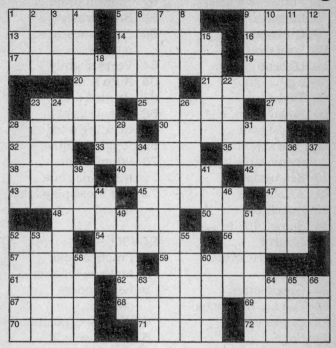

29 Sweet potato
31 Hill, to a Boer
34 One of Barrie's Darlings
36 Garnishes, in a way
37 Colors
39 Explorer Johnson
41 ". . . ay, there's the __"
44 Cry out sharply
46 Cut prices

49 Some files
51 Choice word
52 Pairs of tires
53 Forster's "A Passage to __"
55 A Perón
58 Pointed arch
60 Org.
63 Gig implement
64 Foofaraw
65 Prefix with lead
66 Eye problem

ACROSS

1 Forsakes a lover
6 Lingerie item
9 Dull speaker
13 Love dearly
14 Habeas corpus, e.g.
15 Tied
16 Royal flush, e.g.
18 Small coin
19 __ Maxwell, memorable hostess
20 Sea birds
21 A Johnson
22 Succinct
24 Something to control
26 Eccentric orbit point
29 Greek letter
31 The Lip of baseball
32 Drives (out)
34 Rage
36 Marry
39 Goes to a higher court
41 La Spezia's locale
43 Spelling __
44 Scandinavian victory god
45 Enervated
46 Ham on __
48 Brass producer: Abbr.
51 Hatching posts
52 Most mature
55 Cow catcher
57 Biblical prophet
58 Embarrass
60 Clytemnestra's mother
64 Veers slightly
65 Auto selling point
67 Pointed arch
68 Obsolescent wedding word
69 Representative
70 Wimp's cousin
71 N.Y. time zone
72 Did these play false notes?

DOWN

1 Practical joke
2 Matinee follower
3 Lea winders' sounds
4 Written exposition
5 Indian weight
6 Hair color
7 Get up
8 Trial at Los Alamos
9 Turned into
10 Conquers
11 French income
12 Come in
14 More inferior
17 An L.B.J. beagle
23 Total holdings
25 Bears and Lions
26 Damascene, e.g.
27 Rome V.I.P.

14

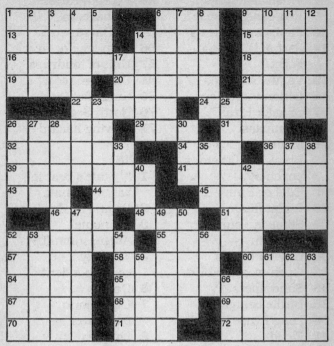

28 U.S.S.R. or U.S.A.,
   in the '80s
30 Broadcast
33 Stallone nickname
35 Josh
37 It will be: Lat.
38 Pops
40 Smash sign
42 Class doctrine
47 Agreed
49 Table wine
50 Impudent

52 Textile type
53 Reflection
54 Western lake
   resort
56 "__ sells
   sea-shells . . ."
59 Weaves' partner
61 Pitcher
62 Sandy tract, in
   England
63 Liberal __
66 Joey of Broadway

ACROSS

1 Musical acronym
6 Red-cased cheese
10 Fancy's antithesis
14 Part of O.S.U. or M.S.U.
15 Vague or Zorina
16 Lotion ingredient
17 Slugger Hank
18 __ impasse
19 Milano money
20 Breakfast fare for a poacher?
22 Edel or Blum
23 Pulpit finale
24 Some are current
26 Restrain
30 City on the Po
32 Open-weave fabric
33 Sandpipers
35 Birdie beater
39 Lengthwise
41 Plead
43 Blackmore outlaw
44 Buddhist monastery
46 Refuse wool
47 Millionaire Hetty
49 Tuberous perennial
51 Dowager
54 This is possibly prehensile
56 City on the Jumna
57 Pluto's realm

63 Pigeon-__
64 Footnote abbr.
65 To have, in Le Havre
66 Irish lake or river
67 Unit of loudness
68 Crimean resort
69 Sires, familiarly
70 North Sea feeder
71 Driving hazard

DOWN

1 "__ tale's best for winter": Shak.
2 Polaris or Rigel
3 "__ nome"
4 At the summit
5 Friendly correspondent
6 Dodge
7 Diplomatic maneuver
8 Limp as __
9 Place for timothy
10 Podiatrist's concern
11 __ and Sedition Acts: 1798
12 Barbizon painter
13 Adolescents
21 Corundum
25 __ armis (with force and arms)
26 Extorted
27 Slots spot
28 __-Chinese

16

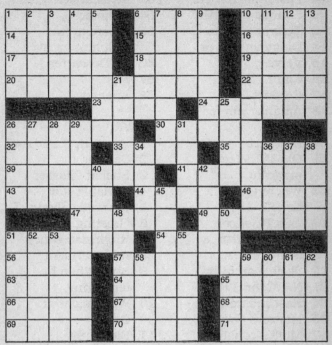

29 Demotes
31 Addict
34 Punta del __,
    Uruguay
36 Earth sci.
37 Sequential
    notes
38 Kett of comics
40 Prefix for dyne
    or drome
42 Lowest point
45 Wrap around

48 Muster
50 Berlin hit
51 Beat Spassky
52 Old market-place
53 Flow
55 Mosquito
58 Contra-bassoon
59 Yale Bowl, e.g.
60 Function
61 Rock: Comb.
    form
62 __ it! (Shucks!)

ACROSS

1 Fastening device
6 Sounds of mirth
10 Type of curtain
14 Diameter halves
15 Verve
16 Calm
17 Coronet
18 An anagram for nail
19 List part
20 Old TV detective program
23 Where to find a panda
24 '80s TV sitcom
25 New Providence Island city
29 Select carefully
31 N.Y.C. or S.F.
34 East Indian vine
35 Mistress Gwyn
37 Mink's cousin
39 Old TV detective program
42 English potter
43 Track shape
44 Skills
45 Letter from Greece
46 Autry or Barry
48 Evaluate
50 Go wrong
51 Appropriate
52 Old TV detectives
59 Novice
60 Colorful perennial
61 Festivals
63 Medical-sch. course
64 __ homo
65 Where to find Dolphins
66 M. Descartes
67 Molt
68 Append

DOWN

1 Scene in "L.A. Law"
2 Secular
3 Shebat follower
4 Variable star
5 Covered gallery
6 Greeting
7 Kirghizian range
8 Arab garment
9 Strengthen by tempering
10 White sight at Dover
11 Biography predecessor
12 Bend
13 Lawn tree
21 As a father, he knew best
22 Mete
25 Oslo citizens
26 Expert
27 Mead research site
28 Glided
29 Garlic portion
30 Armbone
31 Cubic meter

18

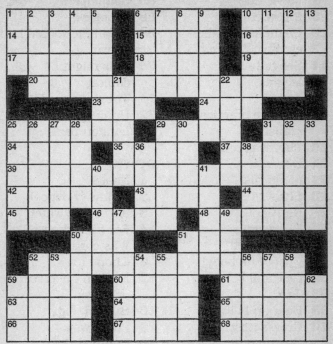

32 Trapper's display
33 Lock
36 Harrow's rival
38 Oolong and hyson
40 Argentine river
41 Rebuffs
47 Banks and Ford
49 Mark of disgrace
50 Ham it up
51 Totaled
52 Since, in Scotland
53 Where to find Qum
54 Prefix for duke or enemy
55 Pleasant French resort
56 Physical strength
57 Buck heroine
58 Entitle
59 Feather's companion
62 Number of angles in a hexagon

ACROSS

1 Movie dog
5 Pillow covers
10 Clemens, Gooden et al.
14 See red
15 Dogma
16 Average
17 Become practical or realistic
20 Phonic preceder
21 Deserve
22 Modernist
23 Shavers
25 Native of Daugavpils
27 Sciatic area
30 __ soul (nobody)
32 Celestial being
36 Jar
38 Bear on high
40 Crow's nest
41 Heston film
44 Honey __ (oscine bird)
45 El __, Tex.
46 Hebrew letters
47 Prepares clams
49 Enlist again, for short
51 Loser to Grant
52 Singer Coolidge
54 Freshly
56 Caviar
59 Bright star
61 Sugar-coated candy
65 Soap opera
68 Ice mass
69 "Old MacDonald had a farm, __"
70 This might be capital
71 Theater award
72 Urgency: Ger.
73 London park

DOWN

1 Basics
2 Chimney deposit
3 It's on the watch
4 Far from drowsy
5 Was conspicuous
6 Chop
7 English queen or princess
8 Bullion, e.g.
9 Puts away
10 Botanist Gray
11 Trite theatrics
12 East wind: Sp.
13 London district
18 Statesman Rusk
19 Ahead, in Aries
24 Honer for razors
26 Wine and dine
27 Some are high
28 __ ease (anxious)
29 Five-sided base
31 __ as the eye can see

10

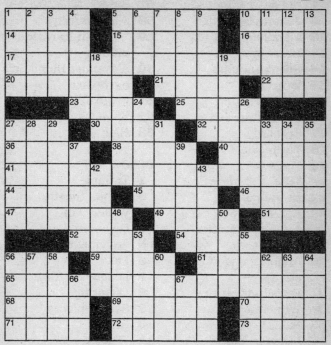

33 Horrify
34 Irk
35 German state
37 Close, in poesy
39 Puzzled
42 Fur for a king
43 Presley hit
48 Packed
50 Saucy
53 Parisian's property

55 "Black Mischief" author
56 Huck's vessel
57 Norway's capital
58 Bond's school
60 Sector
62 Neutral hue
63 Okla. city
64 Feudal underling
66 "__ There," 1954 song
67 Author Yutang

ACROSS

1 "Ici on __ français"
6 Johann Sebastian __
10 Mandible
13 Hautboys
14 Regular: Comb. form
15 Corrida sound
16 Toward the stern
17 Jeopardy
18 Weep aloud
19 Yeats work, with "The"
22 Branch of sci.
23 Apr. and Nov.
24 "__ Rosenkavalier"
25 Linger
26 August's shooting stars
31 Paris legislature
34 Withered
35 Pluck
36 "The Playboy of __": Synge
39 Cupid
40 Plays on words
41 Ph.D. hurdle
42 Yehudi and Hephzibah
44 Use a crowbar
45 Condition: Suffix
46 Part of U.S.D.A.
47 Thus, to Burns
50 "A Portrait of the __ Man": Joyce
55 Turkish title
56 Pursue stealthily
57 Silly
58 Moroccan city
59 "__ of Endearment," hit film
60 Alexander Hamilton's birthplace
61 Football support
62 Sp. miss
63 Hail

DOWN

1 Trample
2 Dublin theatre
3 Writer Dahl
4 Departed
5 Judgment
6 Plot
7 Longfellow town
8 Offspring
9 Sacred places
10 Banter
11 "Thanks __!"
12 Network
14 Chooses
20 Gear tooth
21 Lady __, a founder of Irish National Theatre
25 Court case
26 Hammer parts
27 Bungles
28 Soprano Petina
29 Cousin of parsley
30 Bases of meas. of value

22

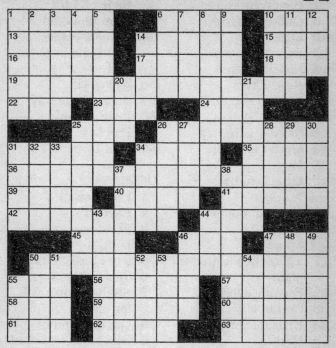

31 Check
32 Honor, in Ulm
33 Light gas
34 Daze
37 Dickens's Miss
   Havisham, e.g.
38 "What's the use
   of __?"
43 Elevators
44 Org. for Corey
   Pavin
46 Invites

47 Urbane
48 Rooney or
   Laurie
49 Perspire, e.g.
50 Pulitzer Prize
   novelist: 1958
51 Demolish
52 Sour
53 College in
   Mich.
54 Rare person
55 P.M. period

ACROSS

1 Haydn sobriquet
5 One-horse town
9 Silent one
13 Borodin prince
14 Kind of power
15 Hit the roof
16 Theater section
17 Carpentry tool
18 Nagy of Hungary
19 Matter for Rollo May
20 Little League "lumber"
22 Rancho rooms
24 Farewell
25 Approve
27 Succeeded at the plate
32 Etching agents
33 Cretan city
34 Huxtable or Rehan
35 Medics
36 Catalogues
37 Mid-21st-century year
38 Bug
39 Compensate, in a way
40 Luce's "The __"
41 Picket's sign
43 Under wraps
44 Polar helper
45 Less experienced
46 Part of a black suit
51 Border

54 G. Eliot drew a Bede on him
55 Diminish gradually
56 Frank's place
57 What one little pig had
58 "No way!"
59 Smooth the way
60 Luge or pung
61 Prophet
62 '60s TV genie

DOWN

1 Rug factor
2 Excited
3 Bouncing toys
4 Land measure
5 Dose for Dobbin
6 Jack of films
7 Shah Jahan's wife, for one
8 G.I. Joe's pineapples
9 Black Sea peninsula
10 A stew base
11 Where 7 Down lived
12 Oval attraction
14 Expand
20 Landon et al.
21 Eye part
23 Gives succor
25 Marconi's interest
26 Incipient oak
27 Seine feeder
28 Pot builder
29 Shark or African bird

24

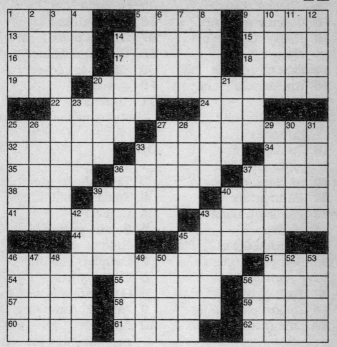

30 Believer in more than half a loaf?
31 Sully
33 Child of TV, e.g.
36 Becomes taut
37 Spassky decision
39 Woody's boy
40 Smash hits
42 Came down cats and dogs
43 Scottish beam
45 More insolent
46 Strikes out
47 Lion
48 Windmill arm
49 Algonquian
50 Pam Shriver's zilch
52 Choice word
53 Appearance
56 Kiki __, rock star

ACROSS

1 Checks
6 Johnny from Ark.
10 Heavy, unmusical clang
14 One more time
15 Ancient Greek city
16 Soon
17 Grayish-white mineral
18 Family
19 Actor Holliday
20 At close quarters
22 Noun suffix
23 Politician Long
24 Ignores
26 Perfumed pad
30 Actress Burstyn
32 __ breve
33 Extinct bird
35 Apportion equally
39 One with a powerful voice
41 Feral
43 Cowboy's "Hello!"
44 "Cómo __ usted?"
46 Number of inches in a span
47 Type of potato
49 Abrupt
51 South American plains
54 Zest
56 Cry of pain
57 Everywhere
63 Official records
64 Theda of silents
65 Separately
66 Noun suffix
67 Wind: Comb. form
68 Tibetan neighbor
69 Ranch employee
70 __ avis
71 Argentine statesman

DOWN

1 Maine port
2 Taj Mahal's site
3 Town NE of Paris
4 Category
5 Scythe part
6 Hide
7 Calmed
8 Connery or O'Casey
9 "Alcina" composer
10 Assume responsibility for
11 Upright
12 __ word
13 What believers fall on
21 Excel
25 "__ we forget . . ."
26 Cummerbund
27 Clef or horn preceder
28 Skein
29 Closely associated
31 Boor

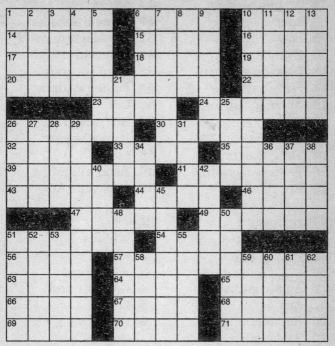

34 Some natural resources
36 During
37 Descartes or Coty
38 British statesman
40 Novice
42 Like the sound of French vowels
45 Norma or Moira
48 Line on a weather map

50 Let go
51 Reluctant
52 Santa __ (fir of Calif.)
53 Affect
55 Andes animal
58 Zola novel
59 Mimic
60 __ Valley, Calif.
61 Type of race
62 Embattled city in July 1944

ACROSS

1 An anagram for spat
5 Low
8 Evaluate
13 Boss on a shield
14 Sail anagram
15 An anagram for shape
16 Noel reversal
17 Tang anagram
18 Prone anagram
19 Result when builders wing it
20 Highway interchanges
22 One of a pair
24 French night
25 An anagram for east
26 Had a taxing job
30 Sackcloth's partner
32 An anagram for times
33 Backward Ira
34 Returning liar
35 __ to (informed)
36 Backward pins
37 Raggedy one
38 Cause anagram
39 Stage anagram
40 Gratuity
42 Spy name

43 Neat anagram
44 Skunk
47 Some truckers
51 Eli anagram
52 Practical
53 Soar anagram
54 Famous Auntie
55 Crape anagram
56 Kine anagram
57 Rain anagram
58 Luges
59 Bend in timber
60 Backward stag

DOWN

1 Whines
2 Sniff
3 Wiping out
4 Not backward
5 Youth
6 Patron saint of Norway
7 Apparent
8 Pertains
9 Bed linens
10 Actress Allgood
11 __ now (currently)
12 Urges
14 Shoelace tag
20 Pacs anagram
21 Outmoded
23 Pare
26 A vestment
27 Calif. city

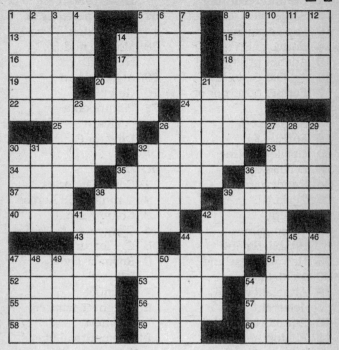

28 Clinton's canal
29 Short swims
30 Backward Lara
31 Yemeni capital
32 Outbursts
35 Monograph
36 See 25 Across
38 Woodworking tools
39 Backward slag

41 Denial anagram
42 An anagram for mores
44 Spirited
45 Draw a bead on
46 Tense anagram
47 Puss anagram
48 Late anagram
49 Rodents
50 Conceited
54 Russian plane

ACROSS

1 Certain recording
5 Seeps
10 Papa's partner
14 Native of Peru
15 Anchor position
16 "__ Old Cow Hand"
17 Former governor of Alaska
18 Roman robe
19 Force
20 Gaelic greeting
23 Office wkr.
24 Concerning
25 "__ la la!"
28 Recede
31 Video-games establishment
33 Hawaiian garland
36 Medicinal plant
39 Attacked with a deterrent
40 Equilibrium point
43 Photographer Adams
44 Minimum follower
45 Asner and Wynn
46 Sound system
48 Memorable impresario __ Hurok
50 Male turkey
51 Louts
54 Kilns
59 Abyss
63 Discovery at Sutter's Mill
65 Northern tribesmen
66 Yugoslav hero: 1892-1980
67 Served perfectly at Wimbledon
68 Moreno and Hayworth
69 Algerian port
70 Go by
71 Picture on a postcard
72 Director Clair

DOWN

1 Counts calories
2 Chunk of 63 Across
3 Column shaft
4 Clergyman
5 Eye feature
6 Room or lay follower
7 Bouquet
8 Weight measures, for short
9 Ancient rival of Athens
10 Southern France
11 Important factor in growth
12 Homo sapiens
13 Picnic pest
21 Kind of dance
22 "__ Rae," Field film
26 "Sweet Smell of Success" author
27 Actress Lamarr
29 Refuse admission
30 Use a bubble pipe

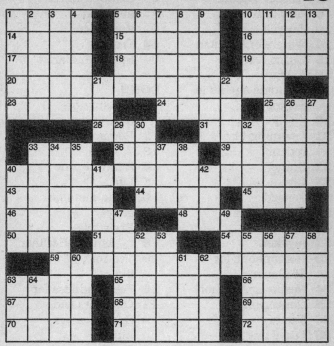

32 Mountain opening
33 Slowly, in music
34 Outfits
35 Ancient road
37 One __ kind
38 Omelet
   requirements
40 Show roster
41 Choose
42 Collectible car
47 Westerns
49 __ Alamos

52 Architectural style
53 Strike down
55 Former N.Y.C.
   meeting place
56 Steeple top
57 Mythical giant
58 Pebble or boulder
60 Bettor's concerns
61 Fatless
62 To be, to Tacitus
63 Opening
64 Wood sorrel

ACROSS

1 Rustler's chasers
6 Black, in Brest
10 Encyclopedia
14 Waters or Merman
15 Cuzco resident
16 Axillary
17 Customs agents in Beijing?
20 __ Tiki
21 Lemming-like rodent
22 Surge
23 Crake
24 Tensed
26 Shoe worn in Aberdeen?
32 Awaken
33 Homophone for 36 Down
34 Response, in short
35 Concerning
36 Factory
38 Leave out
39 __ tai, rum drink
40 Penn of films
41 Critical
42 Mohammedan warriors?
46 Chaplet
47 Summer quaffs
48 Luigi's love
51 Third man
52 Keen in Killarney
55 Small cars in Sasebo?
59 Sci. course
60 Bitter
61 Follow a Child direction
62 Function
63 Trudge
64 Spandau diarist

DOWN

1 Measure of trouble?
2 Roman emperor
3 Tibia
4 E.M.K. is one
5 Lift
6 Dark, metallic alloys
7 Erstwhile
8 "__ bin ein Berliner"
9 "Norma __," Field film
10 Feel fondness for
11 Olive for Ovid
12 Sports-caster Albert
13 Celt
18 Ellerbee's "And __ Goes"
19 Rustic
23 Rambler
24 After that
25 Help a hood
26 Underwater detector
27 Feudal assembly
28 Sail briskly
29 Range
30 Elements

31 Royal Italian name
32 Narrow cleft
36 Ring
37 Lovers' __
38 Operatic baron
40 Chased woman
41 Eternal
43 White ester
44 Caught
45 Parisian perception
48 Discordant

49 __ War (great racehorse)
50 October's gem
51 Aviating prefix
52 Hint for a hawkshaw
53 Plexus
54 Flemish waterway
56 Sixth sense, for short
57 Earth's star
58 Faucet

ACROSS

1 Chutzpah, in the extreme
5 Atlantis proprietor
9 Dwell on tediously
13 Fugitive's moniker
15 Egyptian goddess
16 G.I.'s transgression
17 Mute bird
18 Caron role
19 W.W. II offshoot
20 Together
22 Dew or rain follower
23 Deserter
24 Mr. Fudd
26 Incantations
30 Railroad flare
32 Exhort
33 Chester __ Arthur
35 Take as one's own
39 Complain
40 "__ Be," Beatles song
42 Medley
43 Rice field
45 Throw a party for
46 Sight in an OPEC land
47 Adds seasoning
49 Enmesh
51 Tremble
53 Actor Voight
54 Former Iranian ruler
55 "__ Rose," Streisand hit
62 What Antofalla might spew
63 Bombay garment
64 Adjective for a seance
65 South Yemen's capital
66 Kiln
67 "There is a __ of love": Blake
68 Hawk
69 Salamander
70 Winter plaything

DOWN

1 Wound
2 Utah resort
3 N.F.L. participant
4 Rendered fat
5 This has "a thousand eyes"
6 Singapore's location
7 "Stop" or "Falling Rocks"
8 Thespians' words with the audience
9 Item from a sib
10 Cognizant
11 Part of a Sikorsky vehicle
12 Noise from a fall
14 Sound o' the pipes
21 Twangy
25 Meadow
26 Pit
27 Malayan canoe
28 "Consarn it!"
29 Acts neighborly

34

30 Clotho et al.	**52**	Place to seek sanctuary
31 Gram or meter	**53**	Knee or elbow
34 A Parisian Bank	**54**	Wend or Croat
36 Designer Cassini	**56**	Building part
37 Bolus	**57**	Stars & Stripes heroes
38 Japanned metalware		
41 Wyo.'s __ Range	**58**	__ and haws
44 Tibetan ox	**59**	Seed covering
48 Concern for a student	**60**	Christie's "Death on the __"
50 Bogotá's location		
51 Hades habitué	**61**	Feat

ACROSS

1 Grouse
5 Supply with new weapons
10 What it takes to tango
13 Bar
14 Attention getting call
15 "__ come?"
16 In disgrace
18 Inspiration for Keats
19 Brochette
20 Some nouns
22 Singles
24 Convinced
25 Shade of purple
28 Math proof initials
31 Has to have
34 Ancient wine jug
35 Garb for a gala
37 Bro. or dau.
38 Medieval fur
39 Salutes
40 Hawaiian port
41 Travel stop
42 Fine parchment
43 Begrudge
44 Cosmetician Lauder
46 Part of a journey
47 Summoned, in a way
48 Sharpen
50 Atlas stat.
52 Dusk
55 Relaxed
59 Meadow
60 Trouble spot
63 __ Lanka
64 At a diner, they're short
65 __ over backward
66 Otologist's concern
67 Fits one within another
68 Desires

DOWN

1 Shank
2 File's partner
3 Girl Friday, e.g.
4 Subsided
5 Bird of fable
6 Plumber's pipe
7 Slept like __
8 Rakes
9 Western arbutus
10 Zane Grey's "The __ Herd"
11 By __ of mouth
12 Possesses
14 __ and hounds
17 Director Clair
21 Rubber tree
23 Cry loudly
25 Capra opus
26 Thicke and Bates
27 Undecided
29 Pearl Buck's "The __"
30 Overwhelming amount

36

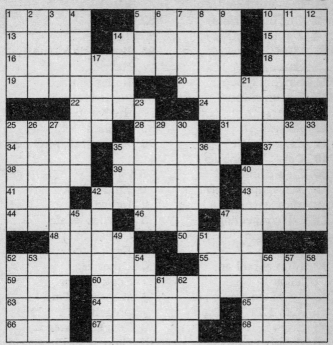

32 Search (into)
33 Manual-training system
35 Tea, in Tours
36 Milit. award
40 Out of this world
42 Pemmican ingredient
45 Ages upon ages
47 A Rose
49 __ nous
51 Resins

52 Other
53 Beth Howland role in "Alice"
54 "__ Little Acre": Caldwell
56 To __ (precisely)
57 Actor Connery
58 Ospreys' cousins
61 Soak, as flax
62 "__ Miniver," 1942 film

ACROSS

1 Cut, in Cheshire
5 One of the rails
9 Water diverter
13 "The __ Love . . . , Kahn song
14 Singing group
15 Patron saint of sailors
16 Record
17 Pa. borough
19 Der __ (Adenauer)
20 Ike's command
21 Newspaper goofs
22 Map feature
24 L-P connection
25 With logic
27 Trouble
32 Kind of ball or fellow
33 "__ of Galilee . . . ": Acts 1:11
35 Erica
36 Weather word
38 Evil spirit
40 One of the Minors
41 Dills of the Bible
43 Topic in a dorm
45 Far: Comb. form
46 Sculptured ornaments
48 Least narrow
50 Loser to H.C.H.
51 Pioneer fur trader
52 Ukrainian bay
56 Edge
57 Latin abbr.

60 Boston commuter area
62 Facet
63 Tempt
64 Boccaccio's "The __ Heart"
65 Nones kin
66 Famed round-the-world solo flier
67 Dashed
68 Aloha State bird

DOWN

1 Kind of jerk
2 Indigo
3 Antilles locale
4 Christian creed
5 Key's middle name
6 Other: Sp.
7 Soak timber
8 Where St. Paul preached
9 Tear's partner
10 Cinders or Fitzgerald
11 "__ a man with . . . "
12 Sub __ (secretly)
14 Like the Cyclops
18 Incensed
23 Sneaky
24 City on the Souris, in N.D.
25 Up to now
26 Bell town
27 Colleague who forsook Paul
28 Farm-improvement org. of the 30's

38

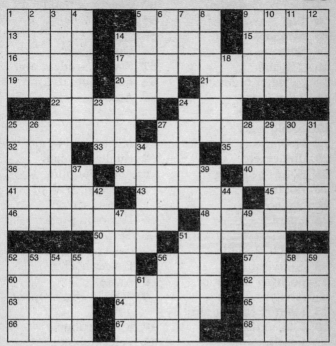

29 Spring time
30 Piggeries
31 Commandment verb
34 King Cyaxares' subjects
37 Way to go: Abbr.
39 Brokaw and Jennings
42 Hide away
44 Pose
47 Annoys

49 Slays
51 Made public
52 Christiania, today
53 Mamie Eisenhower's maiden name
54 Large kangaroo
55 Watch part
56 Memorization method
58 Yemeni seaport
59 __-majesté
61 Occur by chance

ACROSS

1 Draw __ on (aim)
6 Bog
10 Emulate Sarah Siddons
13 __ firma
14 __ Major or Minor
15 John Irving protagonist
17 Skulduggery
19 Hebrew dry measure
20 Juillet, etc.
21 Sonny's sibling
22 Bouquet
23 Nidus
25 Insipid
29 Russian collective
31 Reach by radio
32 __ de France
33 Follower of first or foreign
35 Literary monogram
36 Citizen Kane's Rosebud
37 Haphazard
41 "With malice toward __ . . ."
42 __ -jongg
43 Light-Horse Harry
44 German river
45 Barrett and Jaffe
47 S. American mammal
51 Without choice
54 The Flintstones' pet
55 Actor Delon
56 Rock salt, e.g.
58 Seventh Greek letter
59 Paris's __ Gauche
60 Sleight of hand
64 Sharp
65 __ the Red
66 Occurrence
67 Sixties' student org.
68 Leaf miner or luna
69 Abates

DOWN

1 Minerva, in Rome
2 Kitchen utensil
3 Actor Borgnine
4 __ Royal, W.W. II aircraft carrier
5 Emerson poem
6 Starlike celestial object
7 Flower holder
8 Invite
9 "The Beggar's Opera" author
10 Kind of phobia
11 Peter Rabbit's tea
12 Shaky one
16 Entreated
18 Wrestling win
22 Gibbon, e.g.
24 Naturalist Edwin Way __
26 Parade biggie
27 Cheat
28 Dutch river
30 Kindled
34 Rum, to some
36 Follower of bed or home

40

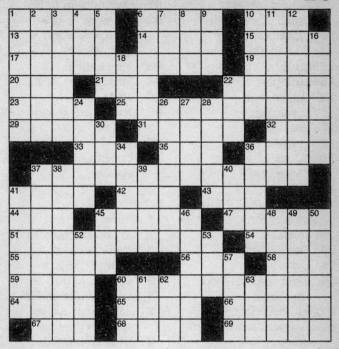

37 Religious
   discourses
38 Subjugated
39 Hindu queen
40 Court call
41 Site of first big U.S.
   airport
45 Rembrandt van __
46 Awkward, lazy
   person
48 "Five Easy __,"
   1970 film

49 Agreeing
50 Some celebrity
   tributes
52 Bank claims
53 Parts of cens.
57 Foil's kin
60 It's fashionably up
   or down
61 Gold, in Genova
62 Op. __ (footnote
   abbr.)
63 Macrogametes

ACROSS

1 School lab
5 Small-scaled trout
9 Played on stage
14 Walter, the drama critic
15 Link part
16 Fabric for a sundress
17 "Dies __"
18 Tony kin
19 Native of ancient Campania
20 Prosaic
23 Four-time O. Henry winner for short stories
24 European gull
28 Eyrie
30 Ester used in food flavorings
31 Violent effort
34 Bonnet, to a London driver
36 __-de-sac
37 Radio quiz show: 1940-49
41 Chemical suffix
42 Countertenor
43 Actress Gold of "Benson"
44 Tole tray, e.g.
47 Louis XV and XVI
49 "__ Eleven," 1960 film
50 Mount
54 Reason for a duel
58 Extremely cold
61 Wine area in Italy
62 ". . . even __ the end of the world": Matt. 28:20
63 Egg-shaped
64 Country, in Córdoba
65 A tide
66 Occupants of some stands
67 Pert
68 Russian news service

DOWN

1 Glides over
2 City on the Hari Rud
3 Speak pompously
4 Sham
5 Household duties
6 Railroad freeloader
7 Start of the Arabic alphabet
8 Offshore hazard
9 Shore bird
10 Share top billing
11 Twitching
12 Guido's high note
13 Place of iniquity
21 Base of printing inks
22 Stage whisper
25 Symbols of authority
26 Needle cases
27 Writer Eudora
29 Pin used as an oarlock

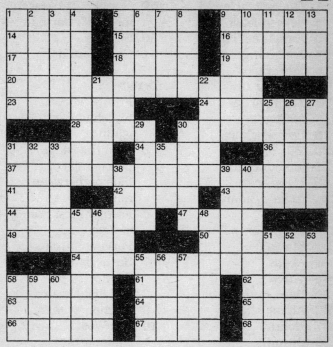

30 Kind of guard
31 Resting: Comb. form
32 A button to push
33 One-seeded fruit: Var.
35 Table scrap
38 Ankles
39 Sect in Pa.
40 Baron's superior
45 Elk
46 Battery parts

48 Crude
51 Octo plus one
52 "__ a Stranger," 1955 movie
53 Stage curtains
55 Valley in Calif.
56 Peter or Paul
57 Of the ear
58 Prepared
59 Topsy's little friend
60 Far from stringent

ACROSS

1 Queen Mab's rod
5 Jewish feast
10 Emulate a lark
14 Lotion ingredient
15 Vibrant
16 Lacking zest
17 The heart of the matter
18 Overwhelmed
20 '80s sitcom
22 Memorandum
23 Prevaricate
24 India's Bihar, Orissa et al.
27 Knight or bishop
32 Stacked
33 Abyss
34 Three __ match
35 Book of the Bible
36 Alpine stream
37 Hokum
38 Swindle
39 Memorable bandleader
41 Recipient of gifts
42 Dürer was one
44 Doxologized
45 Witch bird
46 World's most common surname
47 Star of 20 Across
53 Made an impression
54 Shipshape
56 Uncovered wagon
57 Accrue
58 Ruin
59 "I took __ to search for God": Carman
60 Serious
61 Coop sound

DOWN

1 Funny fellow
2 Finished hang gliding
3 Raid the fridge
4 Lessenings of tension between nations
5 Former First Family of Egypt
6 Parisian pupil
7 Sutherland or Scotto
8 Novelist Hunter
9 Auction events
10 Old West transports
11 __ of allegiance
12 Home of the Cyclones
13 Carmine
19 Use of the second person
21 Princetonian or Yalie
24 Seattle's __ Needle
25 Shakespearean misanthrope
26 "Take Me __," 1959 song

44

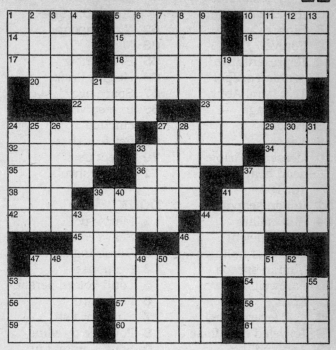

27 Professorship
28 Lagomorph
29 Tumulus
30 It starts in janvier
31 Stark follower
33 Pomander
37 Purchased
profusely
39 Marriage
proclamation
40 Emulates Earhart
41 Euphemistic curse

43 Snow in Tampa, e.g.
44 More stentorian
46 Stassen's "__ I
Stand"
47 Gunsight
48 Pearl Mosque site
49 Slots spot
50 Flog
51 Lough __, in Ireland
52 Incidental
53 Sarnoff's co.
55 Gob's swab

ACROSS

1 "__ Theme" from the Zhivago film
6 Singer Coolidge
10 Forever __ day
14 Representative
15 Arabian seaport
16 Test item: Abbr.
17 Parsonage
18 Peddle
19 Vases
20 Horse in a triple dead heat: June 10, 1944
22 Italian seaport
24 Stiff collars
26 Most ancient
27 Bird that imitates human speech
30 Farewell, in France
32 __ Z (everything)
33 Traveled on a float
35 Applaud
39 Talons
41 Goal; objective
42 Make amends
43 Singer Turner
44 Track wins
46 Compass pt.
47 Habituate
49 Okla. Indians
51 __ Handicap: June 10, 1944
54 More certain
56 Friendly
58 Horse in a triple dead heat: June 10, 1944
62 Nincompoop
63 Medley
65 Before now
66 Height: Prefix
67 Space agcy.
68 In reserve, or cinched
69 For fear that
70 Insect pest
71 Desert shrub

DOWN

1 Mary's pet
2 Seaweed extract
3 Gambling city
4 Response
5 Loud-voiced persons
6 Poe's bird
7 Suffix or fish
8 Portable dwelling
9 Sci-fi automaton
10 Site of triple dead heat
11 Hospital worker
12 Fender mishaps
13 Something of value
21 Jot
23 __ du Diable
25 Lampoons
27 Treaty
28 King of the Huns
29 Horse color
31 G.O.P.'s opposition

46

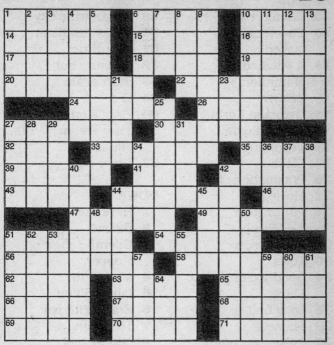

34 Impartial
36 Yearn
37 Comedienne Meara
38 Church seats
40 Horse in a triple dead heat: June 10, 1944
42 Property-tax person
44 The event on June 10, 1944, was a seven-__ race
45 Corrida beast

48 Bird's beak
50 Poisonous gas
51 Intrigue
52 Soap plant
53 Disorders
55 German sub
57 Verve
59 One
60 "__ homo!"
61 Swarm
64 "The Lady __ Tramp"

ACROSS

1 Mop
5 Canter, etc.
10 Chesterfield or blazer
14 A Mitchell plantation
15 Bizarre
16 Gymnast Korbut
17 Enthusiastic
18 Beginning
19 Close
20 Pragmatic person
22 Movie fare
24 Put to good __
25 "__ Macabre"
26 Steeler score
30 Tows
34 Good-looking man: Slang
35 Lode find
36 Phone
37 Pulver, for one: Abbr.
38 Capistrano visitor
40 Kind of angle
41 He cometh onstage
43 Gehrig or Groza
44 Elem.-sch. head
45 Televised again
46 Reduce in importance
48 Tree exudation
50 Also
51 High __

54 Gettysburg event: 1863
58 Italian wine city
59 Vegas headliner
61 A Guthrie
62 Measure out
63 Start again
64 Fed
65 Plant's origin
66 They are, in Tijuana
67 Diner sign

DOWN

1 Have the lead
2 Billow
3 Operatic show stopper
4 Misfortune
5 Pillow filling
6 Em or Pittypat
7 That thing's
8 Mining tool
9 Mother or Anya
10 Hide
11 Butterine
12 Gelling substance
13 Mountain lake
21 Somewhat: Suffix
23 "Shucks!"
25 Talk about repeatedly
26 Churchill's "__ Finest Hour"
27 Part of a pound

24

28 Indy name
29 "__ pro nobis"
31 Very
32 Sensational
33 Backbone
36 NASA arithmetic
38 More rational
39 Moo
42 No longer single
44 Apportion
46 Postprandial chore

47 Divinity
49 "__ bleu!"
51 Spade and Hill
52 Words of understanding
53 Diminutive ending
54 Neighborhood
55 Writer Bombeck
56 Wood strip
57 Pearl Buck book
60 Aardvark's tidbit

ACROSS

1 Solidify
5 Kind of box
9 Variegated chalcedony
14 Biblical prophet
15 Dramatist from Kan.
16 Punctuation mark
17 Burgess beast
19 Stratus, e.g.
20 Killarney-to-Blarney dir.
21 Verb ending
22 They got away
24 P.M. item for a hostess
26 Singer Della
27 Void
29 Peddler
33 Was eminent
36 Whirling vapor
38 Author Vidal
39 Jaunty
40 __ Baba
41 Heavy literature
42 Kind of door
43 Hadrian's 554
44 Place for a hen party
45 "Sorrow chang'd to __ . . . ": Shak.
47 Spot seen on Mars
49 Actor Lloyd
51 Architectural wing
55 Suppress
58 Feel below par
59 Old English coin
60 __ Melba
61 Kind of contract
64 Ethyl acetate, e.g.
65 Legendary vessel
66 Own
67 Task
68 Stingy
69 Companion of terminer

DOWN

1 King of France: 987-96
2 Emulate a jester
3 Country called Chosen by Japanese
4 Letters for a mind reader
5 Nap
6 Tale starter
7 Gone by
8 Phoebe
9 Impeach
10 Nugget layer
11 Tonic base
12 Trip
13 Companion of odds
18 Tetched
23 Assess
25 Cartoon feline
26 Town in Pa.
28 Actress Patricia
30 Major-__

31 Prill and stibonite
32 Remainder
33 N.Y. and S.F., e.g.
34 Leander's beloved
35 Actinal
37 Callas was one
41 Infielder Manny __
43 Expunge
46 Stick
48 Popeye, e.g.
50 Indo-Iranian
52 "__ a Shepherd,"
poem by St. Teresa
53 Treasure __
54 Zealous
55 Arch.'s drawing
56 Network
57 VIII, to Ovid
58 Stonewort
62 Homophone for heir
63 Agcy. promoting
physical well-being

ACROSS

1 Part of an M.O.
6 Sear
10 Coin of Colombia
14 Mistreat
15 Gigantic
16 Bakery worker
17 Casino game
18 Like some vaccines
19 City in Rumania
20 "__ here!"
21 The Scooter
24 Cut wool
26 Utters in Br'er Fox jargon
27 Canopy
29 Tried again
33 Place for a watch
34 Salad ingredients, for short
35 N.A.A.C.P., e.g.
37 Eye parts
38 What fielders shag
39 A Met star in 1969
40 __ Anne de Beaupré
41 Pituitary, e.g.
42 Baseballer's shoe part
43 Soon, to Spenser
45 What Bernhardt trod
46 Morning lawn sight
47 Feast of Lots
48 An artful Dodger: 1940-58
53 Athos, to Porthos

56 He played Pierce
57 Author Jaffe
58 Flagged
60 Lecher's look
61 Jannings of filmdom
62 Banal
63 Give temporarily
64 Some June heroes
65 Dolts

DOWN

1 Charts
2 Orchestral member
3 A teammate of 48 Across
4 Employ
5 Eve's tempter
6 Loft group
7 Fling
8 Gelling agent
9 Chow chow, etc.
10 Public square, in Torino
11 Neutral color
12 Stock-exchange position
13 Church calendar
22 Crone
23 Snorer's letters
25 Villain's greeting
27 Hole-making tools
28 Pen
29 Repentant
30 Supplemented, with "out"

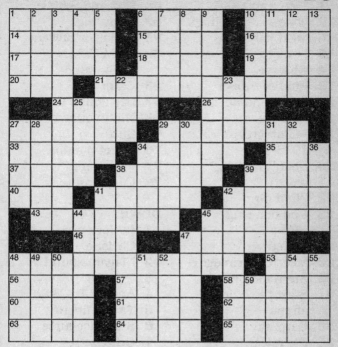

31 Mantle teammate

32 Terror

34 Auel's "The __ of the Cave Bear"

36 Understands

38 Blossomed

39 Jai __

41 Kind of club that might give hits

42 Mrs. King

44 Famous Confessor

45 Steinbeck's erratic vehicle

47 Rings out

48 Grow dull

49 Robert __

50 Actress Barbara

51 Capital of Italia

52 Writer Bagnold

54 Measure out

55 Bad day for Caesar

59 D.C. agcy.

26

53

ACROSS

1 "To __ and a bone . . .": Kipling
5 Meat jelly
10 __ mater
14 Observe
15 Kind of rubber
16 Baltic and Adriatic
17 Defense org.
18 A diamond M.V.P.: 1958-59
20 Noah's landing place
22 Wind dir.
23 End of a ring count
24 Elated
26 Mecca pilgrimage
28 Supreme Being
31 Start the bidding afresh
35 Carp kin
36 Chemical compound
38 "__ Go the Boats?": R.L.S.
39 Birthright possessor
40 Kind of boom
42 Ancient ointment
43 Synthetic fiber
45 Hindu hero
46 Col. and sgt.
47 __ quo
49 Painter's device
51 Louise or Turner
53 A Yugoslav
54 Hirt and Smith
57 Ruby, e.g.
58 Dallas or Stevens
62 An M.V.P.: 1954, 1965
66 Carol
67 Lily Pons's forte
68 Hindu queen
69 Stuff
70 Sweet potatoes
71 Fasteners
72 Coop group

DOWN

1 Pavlova or Christie
2 Niagara sound
3 "__ boy!"
4 An M.V.P.: 1980
5 Textile fibers
6 Sun. discourse
7 Criticize
8 Dubliners
9 Julius or Sid
10 __ rule (generally)
11 Fasting period
12 Manufacture
13 N.A.A.C.P., e.g.
19 Moisten overnight
21 __ mode
25 Giver
27 An M.V.P.: 1970, 1972
28 Quartz

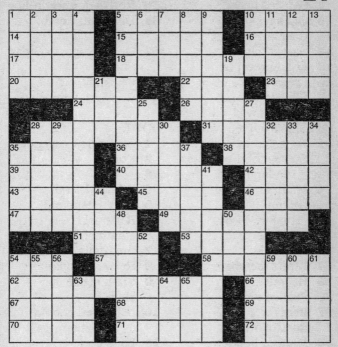

29 Wreck, in Madrid
30 Jaffe and Barrett
32 Tranquility
33 Miscue
34 Calmer and Rorem
35 Future Eng. king
37 Walks lamely
41 Pets
44 Louis, in Pisa
48 Expresses contempt

50 Sculpture, e.g.
52 Jordan's capital
54 Absent
55 Money in Milano
56 Svelte
59 Knowledge
60 Incline
61 Mendicant's request
63 __ Vegas
64 Memorabilia
65 Slangy agreement

ACROSS

1 Singer Turner
5 Old saying
10 Caspian seaport
14 Saroyan hero
15 Legal precepts
16 Protection
17 Shchedrin and Shostakovich
20 Ship's curved plank
21 Tones down
22 Subject of the eddas
23 __-de-lance
24 Milan or Peking ending
25 "The Fire-bird" composer
33 Piano key
34 Lepus members
35 Hasten
36 Festive event
37 Item for Rostropovich
38 Marx or Malden
39 Washington bill
40 Russian girl's name
41 Slavic gymnasts' society
42 "Scheherazade" composer
45 First year after BC
46 Wedding words
47 Harass
50 Courage
53 Coin in Kiev: abbr.
56 "Cinderella" ballet composer

59 Asian sea
60 Ruth's mother-in-law
61 Different: Comb. form
62 Dr. Zhivago, to Omar Sharif
63 Chekhov, e.g.
64 Russian, for one

DOWN

1 Soviet news agency
2 Press
3 __ blue
4 French friend
5 Rubinstein and Rodzinski
6 Channel
7 Amaryllis's cousin
8 Ruby and opal
9 Sixth sense, for short
10 "Children should __ . . ."
11 Long period
12 Soprano __ Te Kanawa
13 Former UN member
18 Corundum
19 Sahara stopover
23 Tribunals
24 Tied
25 Russian ruler
26 Jewish folklore figure
27 Show gratitude
28 Proportion
29 Bellowing

56

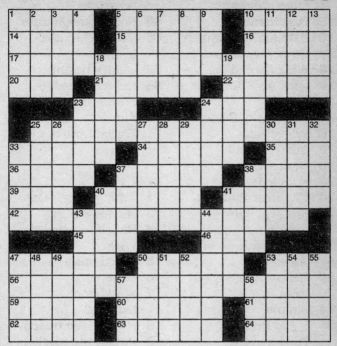

30 Military hat
31 Russian ballet
32 Cheer
33 Borodin's Prince
37 Hopalong Cassidy portrayer
38 "Mikado" role
40 Ray
41 Opera by 42 Across
43 Not married
44 Penetrate slowly

47 Glinka's "A Life for the __"
48 Aviation word form
49 Russian river
50 Bridge
51 Luth. or Episc.
52 Man, in Mantua
53 Brooklet
54 Bartók
55 City in the Ukraine
57 Actress Balin
58 Scale notes

ACROSS

1 More plucky
6 Dissonant
10 Fare for Miss Muffet
14 Oil or Oyl preceder
15 Wide-spread
16 Lock inventor Linus __
17 Vampire of folklore
18 Protection
19 Austen novel
20 Dentist?
23 Fulfilled
24 City near Phoenix
25 Surgical light beams
27 Command
31 Joiner?
33 Genus of evergreen trees
34 Simple
36 "__ to Be You," 1924 song
39 Marsh heron
41 Tools for swindlers?
43 Pelvic bones
44 Actress-writer Chase
46 Baby powder
47 Squabble
49 Allen and Herman
51 Guadalajara gala
53 Deviate
55 __ Deco
56 Carpenter's libation?
62 Punjabi prince

64 One of the brassicas
65 Roman magistrate
66 College founded in 1440
67 Glades beginner
68 Della or Pee Wee
69 Fiscal concern
70 Filmdom V.I.P.'s
71 Zigged from a course

DOWN

1 "The __ Bug": Poe
2 Having wings
3 Rodolfo's beloved
4 Wicked
5 Kingdoms
6 Spheres
7 Workbench bafflers?
8 Have __ (be upset)
9 Put on the market again
10 Ex follower
11 Shark who is Mike's boss?
12 Gantry or Fudd
13 Irish poet-playwright
21 __ maid
22 Diameter halves
26 Gets at it
27 Moves like a cork on water
28 Famed pen name

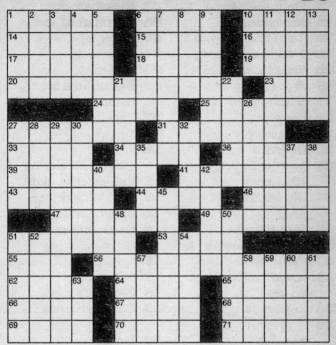

29 Backstabber's
   act?
30 Added attractions
32 Jan van __,
   Flemish painter
35 Indigo
37 Friend in a fray
38 Milit. medals
40 Bridge positions
42 Hemmed and __
45 Honest planer?
48 Gave the ax to

50 Planetarium
51 Got along
52 Steaming
54 Wide-mouthed
   pitchers
57 Sitarist Shankar
58 Concept
59 "A __ From the
   Bridge": A. Miller
60 Otherwise
61 Bulrush, e.g.
63 Carpenter __

ACROSS

1 Plant disease
5 Armbones
10 Bat a gnat
14 Trademark
15 Red Sox rightfielder
16 Prong
17 "Family Ties" son
18 Puppet
20 Shopkeeper
22 Defeated
23 "__ She Sweet?": 1927 song
24 Old MacDonald's place
25 Was clement
28 Felt amazement
32 Criticize
33 Room's adornment scheme
35 Author Jong
36 "__ Death," Grieg passage
38 Street show
40 Card game for three
41 Disgrace
43 Bellini opera: 1831
45 Homophone for air
46 Annual event in Boston
48 Flora
50 Korean statesman
51 Spirit
52 Share the lead
55 Difficult to change or break
59 Obvious
61 Hawaiian city
62 Egyptian dancer
63 At large
64 Microwave
65 Nitwits
66 Distributed bit by bit
67 Take it easy

DOWN

1 Close with a bang
2 Cabbagelike plant
3 Antiquing device
4 Freight-train part
5 Court officer, at times
6 __-garde
7 Scoot
8 Zoology suffix
9 Certain barometric line
10 Liners
11 German champion figure skater
12 Help to create a pot
13 Harold of comics
19 Courage
21 Sped
24 Word with way or sea
25 Sudden spell of activity
26 Former Turkish title
27 Lend __ (listen)

28 Andalusian city
29 Compare
30 Cocteau's "Le Grand __"
31 Dorm topics
34 Kayak or birchbark
37 Show-offs
39 Engaged
42 Allen or Frome
44 Comedian King

47 Proclaim
49 Secure
51 Cancel
52 Auditors, for short
53 Spicy stew
54 Coarse hominy
55 Celebrity
56 In person
57 Pub drinks
58 "__ Tread on Me"
60 US-Ont. canals

ACROSS

1 Bilko, briefly
4 Butler's wife
9 Ricochet
13 Field
15 Wisent
16 __ down (subdue)
17 It opened on Broadway Dec. 30, 1948
19 College in New Rochelle
20 Operating at a loss
21 Thelonious and family
23 TV's "The __ Squad"
24 Group dance
25 Engage
29 Halloween treat
32 Farthest from the pin
33 Street show
34 Expression of disgust
35 Counterweight
36 Jabs
37 Prop for Alice on TV
38 Gee-tar's cousin
39 Not live
40 Somber
41 River in W Turkey
43 Gas-station word
45 Queue
46 Abbr. akin to alias
47 __ down (loses weight)
48 Inclined to bite
53 Lament
54 Trickery
56 Fortune
57 Roman magistrate
58 Martha from Butte
59 Annoys
60 Full
61 Threefold: Comb. form

DOWN

1 H.H. Munro's pen name
2 Put on a happy face
3 Poor student's bane
4 An Olivier co-star: 1939
5 Went on a long walk
6 "__ tale's best for winter": Shak.
7 Tommy follower
8 Showy flowers
9 Parsimonious
10 Bird also called laughing jackass
11 Travel-section listing
12 Kind of shooter
14 Cheroot residue
18 Written reminder
22 Wave, to a Frenchman
24 Felt concern
25 An O'Neal
26 Not asleep
27 Actress in "Family Plot"
28 Where the cornea is

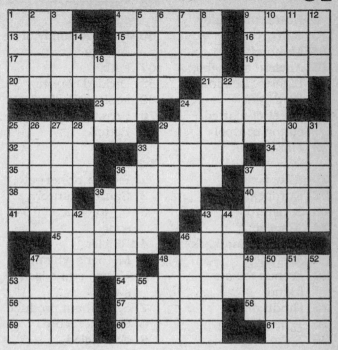

29 Encrusts
30 Once more
31 Nursery __
33 Used a lariat
36 Pastors' concerns
37 Its ctr. is a bull's-eye
39 Dallas Cowboys, e.g.
42 Bartenders' concerns
43 Gave approval
44 Creator of Mammy Yokum

46 Talus
47 Like some grapes
48 In a __ (agitated)
49 One less than a bogey
50 __ the finish
51 Kind of terrier
52 "Jezebel" actress on TV: 1950's
53 Half of MMCII
55 Susan Hayward film: 1961

ACROSS

1 Chatter
6 Entrapment ploy
10 Stark
14 Mountebank
15 Ancient strongbox
16 Lamb's pseudonym
17 Divergent
18 Sheet of matted cotton or wool
19 Mardi Gras follower
20 Take a risk
22 European sled
23 Songbird
24 "Caveat __"
26 London landmark
30 Assume
32 French female friend
33 Hindu dress
35 Type of wheat
39 Town crier
41 Western hill
43 "__ of Two Cities"
44 Samoan seaport
46 Deserve
47 Fritter away
49 Described grammatically
51 Effective
54 Yuletide
56 What accomplices do
57 Strikes a response
63 Interlock
64 Kind of hygiene
65 Early French comedy
66 Famous family of Ferrara
67 Path
68 Divided country
69 Look lustfully
70 Permits
71 Better

DOWN

1 Fiddler or hermit
2 Canter leisurely
3 "__ in Calico," 1946 song
4 Ringlet
5 Mother's whistler
6 Heavy, one-edged sword
7 S. Graham product
8 Official record
9 Entangled
10 Salad ingredient
11 Alaskan Indian
12 Starr among the Beatles
13 Gourmand or gourmet
21 Medieval merchant guild
25 Cogitate
26 Small cake
27 "__ a man with seven wives"
28 Colorado feeder

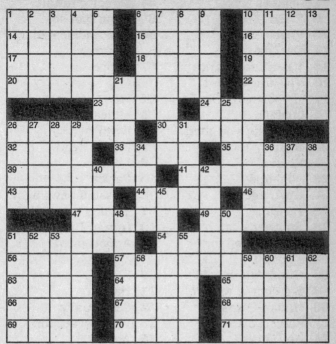

29 Leader
31 Unless, to Cicero
34 Sci. subject
36 Greek vowels
37 Wisdom
38 Look after
40 Connote
42 What some victors break
45 Banner
48 Promenade
50 "Seward's Folly"

51 Desert ruminant
52 Overweight
53 Beau __ (magnanimous action)
55 Eyes amorously
58 Dies __
59 What Clancy lowered
60 Being: Fr.
61 Property right
62 Plumbum

ACROSS

1 Jellifies
5 Place
10 Phase
14 Declare
15 Valentino's dance
16 Volcanic output
17 He portrayed Tevye onstage
19 The yoke's on them
20 Saint __ cross
21 Realm
23 Jimjams
24 Govt. agency
25 Perfume
28 Sniggler's catch
30 Provide food for a fee
35 Guadalajara gold
36 Signifying, with "of"
38 Hanks-Gleason film: 1986
41 Ancestors
42 __ out (supplement)
43 Father of Indira Gandhi
44 Xenon, e.g.
45 Metal fastener
47 "Norma __"
49 "__ the ramparts ..."
50 Upset
54 Turtleneck, e.g.
58 Anderson of "WKRP"
59 Nuclear explosion hot spot
62 Dobbin's fare
63 Laszlo Loewenstein
64 Director Kazan
65 Prior spouses
66 __ out (defeated narrowly)
67 Judge

DOWN

1 Mideast's __ Strip
2 Level
3 Manor head
4 Rapiers
5 Packs
6 Russian news agcy.
7 Tolkien creature
8 Iron or Bronze
9 Apportioned sparingly
10 Slush
11 Hack
12 Perpetually
13 Window section
18 Allot
22 Neighbor of Hong Kong
24 Spark makers
25 Schwarzenegger role
26 Jagged
27 Indentation
28 Hire
29 Minneapolis suburb
31 Unit of pressure: Abbr.
32 Track official
33 Elicit

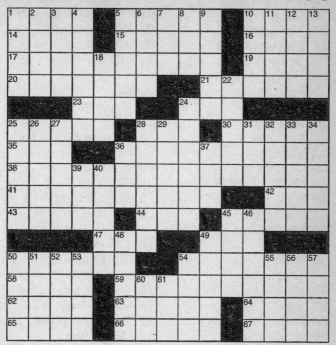

34 Extend a subscription
36 Neighbor of Ill.
37 Lab measures: Abbr.
39 "Leave __ to heaven": Shak.
40 Harden
45 Acorn, e.g.
46 Off one's rocker
48 Fish
49 Possessed

50 Type of gin
51 Fraud
52 Feed the kitty
53 Osculate
54 Certain
55 Beginning for vision
56 Lake seen at Lakewood, Ohio
57 Wander
60 Reel's partner
61 Assoc.

ACROSS

1 Bamboozle
5 Old hat
10 Flutie was one
14 Iridescent gem
15 Bay window
16 Dashiell contemporary
17 Steve
20 Tiny colonist
21 Loses color
22 Facilitates
23 Sonny's sibling
24 "Bali __," 1949 song
25 Steve
33 Buckeye
34 Contents of Alice's pool
35 "Sail __ Union . . . !": Longfellow
36 Killer whale
37 Type of beet
38 Make cardigans
39 Sch. affiliate
40 Seven, in Sevilla
41 Free from frost
42 Steve
45 "Blessed __ the meek . . . "
46 Suffix with depend
47 She wrote "My Friend Flicka"
50 Sometimes it's clear
53 "Whiffenpoof" song ender
56 Steve
59 Very, in Versailles
60 Singer Kay of "Stop the Music"
61 Opposite of aweather
62 Cummerbund
63 All tuckered out
64 Tall flower, for short

DOWN

1 Copperfield's first wife
2 Fairy tale's second word
3 Covenant
4 Tooth wearer
5 Dead Sea product
6 Russian body of water
7 Paddock papa
8 Works on a sampler
9 Inventor Whitney
10 Complain about
11 Cupid, to Plato
12 Liliaceous plant
13 Beatty film
18 Variety, to life
19 Comes closer
23 A portico
24 Adamantine
25 Start of some books
26 Peruvian sun worshiper
27 Waters or Merman
28 Ranch in "Giant"
29 Famed baseball player or poet
30 Pick-me-up
31 In reserve

68

34

32 Hemidemi-
semiquaver
33 "Cheese it, the __!"
37 Highly glazed
fabric
38 Lear's loyal servant
40 Block of glacial ice
41 Fender flaws
43 Showy
44 Become indignant
47 Halloween mos.
48 Israeli dance

49 College town in
Iowa
50 Freshwater food
fish
51 "This one is __!"
52 Capital of South
Yemen
53 Liberty __
54 Sector
55 Like Methuselah
57 __ Vegas
58 Something to tote

ACROSS

1 Shy
6 Play parts
10 "Sweeney __," 1979 Broadway hit
14 Tyrrhenian feeder
15 Snare
16 Mimic
17 Solo
18 Fork part
19 Garden access
20 Loafer
23 "__ Misérables"
24 Tress
25 Widows' inheritances
27 Confuses
31 Follows
33 __ gras
34 Satisfy fully
36 "__ bleu!"
39 Surveyor's instrument
41 Importune
43 Island group north of Tonga
44 Actress Garr
46 "With the blue ribbon __"
47 Trial
49 Kindly
51 Thin layer
53 Needle parts
55 Unusual
56 Revere occupation

62 Pinball machine word
64 Array in a pool hall
65 Famous cow
66 Lamb
67 "Thousand Days" queen
68 McKinley's birthplace in Ohio
69 Take out
70 Lip
71 One of a baseball trio

DOWN

1 Male partygoer
2 Hawaiian city or bay
3 One-sixth drachma
4 Tear
5 Soprano
6 Athenian
7 Fair play
8 Place for cogitation
9 Does 75
10 Label
11 Like a girasol
12 Hold back
13 Shift or sheath
21 Actor Ernesto: 1829-96
22 Yank out of bed
26 Irritate; fray
27 P.M.'s
28 A Copperfield
29 Mae West role

70

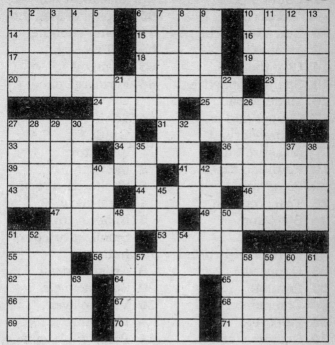

30 Poe girl
32 Never, to Keats
35 "__ boy!"
37 Inveigh
38 Feminine suffix
40 Vic's spouse et al.
42 Its capital is Niamey
45 N.F.L. groups
48 The true heaths
50 Ancient ascetic

51 Cast a ballot
52 Roman official
54 Affirmatives
57 Moon goddess
58 Year in Macbeth's reign
59 Man, for one
60 Row
61 Dame Myra
63 R.L.S. contemporary

ACROSS

1 Caldwell's "Tobacco __"
5 Con man's scheme
9 Insensitive
14 Give the eye
15 Spanish appetizer
16 Made public
17 Copper and iron
18 Hebrew dry measure unit
19 Fountain fizzes
20 Persevere
23 Toast topping
24 Singleton
25 Endured
28 More hard-hearted
33 Opposed
34 Promote
35 Common verb
36 Persevere
40 Cochlea's site
41 Reclines
42 Mine entrance
43 Answers
45 Analyzes grammatically
47 Toronto's prov.
48 Wampum
49 Persevere
56 Japanese gateways
57 Coup d'__
58 Belgian river

59 Taken __ (disconcerted)
60 Capital of Manche
61 Castor's mother
62 Gift receiver
63 Drain pit
64 Formerly, once

DOWN

1 Castle for Kasparov
2 Monster
3 Sheltered, at sea
4 Tyrannical
5 In one's cups
6 Small featured role
7 Imitates
8 Artist Chagall
9 Steel helmets
10 Vibes player Hampton
11 Pakistani language
12 Tide type
13 QB's goals
21 Señor's shout
22 Theater audience
25 "Star Wars" beam
26 Architectural pillars
27 Budges
28 Becomes indifferent
29 Howard and Reagan

72

36

30 Praises
31 Pyle or Ford
32 Takes five
34 Intrepid
37 Gold rush site: 1890's
38 Silverheels role
39 Gutter garnish
44 Men in blue
45 Spinning toy
46 Swiss river

48 Sacred song
49 King of the road
50 Algerian seaport
51 Promontory
52 "__, Brute!"
53 Employer
54 Buntline and Beatty
55 Mild oath
56 Urchin

ACROSS

1 Salver
5 Comic Wilson
9 Family name in rock
13 Ship's creation at sea
14 Occupation
15 First floor apartment
16 Words from John Lyly
19 Second highest pinochle card
20 Gold of "Benson"
21 Tooth: Comb. form
22 Price
23 Fashionable resort
24 Words from George Herbert
31 Event for Irwin
32 Carol
33 Utter
35 Superman
36 Throb
38 TV's Hawkeye
39 Historic time
40 Flatfish
41 Twins or socks, e.g.
42 Words from Robert Burton
47 Corn unit
48 Bufo
49 Concerning
52 Bright
54 Torah repository
57 Words from F.D.R.
60 Give off, as light
61 Puccini heroine
62 Poker stake
63 Disavow
64 Kitchen or major suffix
65 Mulligan, e.g.

DOWN

1 Taunt
2 Deserve
3 Related
4 Nod's meaning
5 Snowman of song
6 Papa of TV's "Mama"
7 In a lazy way
8 Foot: Comb. form
9 As __ gold
10 __ many words
11 "I've __ to London . . . "
12 Borscht ingredient
14 Contort
17 Cupid
18 Actor in "Fiddler . . . "
22 Penny
23 Snick and __
24 Jab
25 Verdi work
26 Mercenary
27 Creek
28 Help!

74

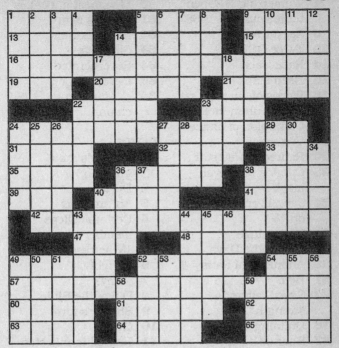

29 Moslem faith
30 Gymnast Comaneci
34 Word with arm or stick
36 __ Clare (nun)
37 Rubber tree
38 Mimicked
40 Gaiters
43 Clemency
44 Golfer's posture
45 Arterial trunk
46 Pro __

49 Filled with reverence
50 Call
51 Moran of "Happy Days"
52 Glaswegian
53 Maximum
54 "__ Misbehavin' "
55 Learning method
56 Recognized
58 Tea anagram
59 Petrol

ACROSS

1 Women's U.S. Open tennis champ: 1968
5 See 51 Across
10 Twice DCL
14 Race track
15 Deep black
16 Words of surprise
17 Actor Auberjonois
18 Champion of dance
19 Veracious
20 Retired tennis star
23 C.P.A.'s employer, maybe
24 Jay Silverheels on TV
25 Uses a luge
27 One of the Days
30 Anouk from Paris
31 Bête __
32 Saved, as one's strength
36 Building addition
37 Bounce back
38 Inner: Prefix
39 Popular
42 A Nobel physicist: 1925
44 Subtle satire
45 __ ball (alert)
46 Where Eugene may be seen
48 Human chaser
51 With 5 Across, Agra edifice
52 Tennis star
57 Made tracks

59 Costar of 46 Down
60 Like most cupcakes
61 Jacob's twin
62 Bay window
63 Show life
64 Reverberated
65 Devon donkey
66 __ Mandlikova, 1985 champ

DOWN

1 Brewer's malt infusion
2 Declare
3 An Andrews
4 Certain college member
5 TV actress Fellows
6 Roughly
7 "Why?"
8 Dill of the Bible
9 Shelley's forte
10 Quip
11 Retired tennis star
12 Retired tennis star
13 Castle a king here
21 Auld lang syne
22 Alaskan city
26 Chalice veil
27 Once more
28 Function
29 King of tennis
30 "And giving __, up the chimney . . . ": Moore
32 Like compact powder

76

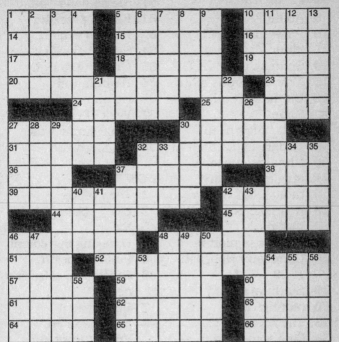

38

33 Pay dirt
34 Man from Tallinn
35 Drop off
37 Reddish brown
40 Bigger than med.
41 Crazy sounding bird
42 Hagar the Horrible's daughter
43 Spin put on a ball
46 "The __ Woman," Linden TV movie
47 Soprano Rosa

48 Queue
49 Auriculate
50 Davis Cup winner: 1976
53 Billy Budd's captain
54 Prefix with chord or meter
55 Mood
56 Historic Spanish town
58 Liked

ACROSS

1 Game fish
5 Abate
10 Purviance of old films
14 Spanish pot
15 Maine campus site
16 Emulate Nevele Pride
17 This "runs deep"
19 Dixieland jazzman Al
20 Himalayan people
21 Magician of early radio
23 Roanoke Island's Virginia
24 Corporate motto
25 Chemistry Nobelist: 1922
28 Stadium sound
30 More recent
33 The Swamp Fox
35 Like some sheep
37 __ atque vale!
38 Scott Hamilton feat
39 Donizetti specialty
41 School gps.
42 Animal: Comb. form
43 __ patriae
44 Star requisite
46 Over
48 Old English letter
50 Concise
51 Carpus
53 Cinders of old comics

55 Lacedaemon
57 Stevenson's island
61 Kappa preceder
62 Petrel's cousin
64 Secluded valley
65 Greeting to Dolly
66 Hentoff and Holman
67 Pack of camels
68 What Eadie was
69 Quaker word

DOWN

1 Petty officer
2 Der __ (Adenauer)
3 Error
4 Dressing ingredient
5 Pullman berth
6 Crossword puzzler's need
7 Bag type
8 "__ Saison en Enfer": Rimbaud
9 Veranda
10 Fuel gas
11 "Abraham Lincoln" playwright: 1918
12 Lille's department
13 Aleutian island
18 Plain, in Spain
22 Clue
24 Aesir defender
25 Astonish
26 Harold II, e.g.
27 Keep afloat via leg action

78

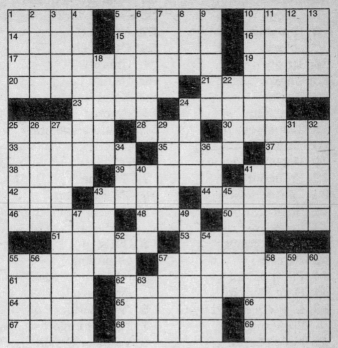

39

29 On the qui vive
31 Linda or Maurice
32 Remainder, in Rennes
34 __ de guerre
36 Made a lap
40 Southey was one
41 Enjoyable
43 Stulm
45 Attorney __
47 Commission
49 Forerunner

52 Dostoyevsky girl
54 Memorable director Mervyn
55 Wind sound
56 Position on a race track
57 Honduran seaport
58 Beehive State
59 Neural network
60 Gaelic
63 Niflheim ruler

ACROSS

1 Chinese nanny
5 Mild oath
9 Erstwhile Russian rulers
14 Tardy
15 Charles Lamb
16 Needing to scratch
17 Cruising
18 Transgressions
19 Faulty car: Slang
20 Doyle's detective
23 French head
24 Matter, legally
25 Start eating
28 In the distance
30 City railways
33 Farewell
34 Fit of pique
35 Genus of olives
36 Mystery solved by 20 Across
39 Male offspring
40 Singer Jerry
41 Ancient port of Rome
42 Ft. Benning, Ga., inst.
43 Weary
44 Shining
45 Bolt's partner
46 Forbidden, in Frankfurt
47 __ Irregulars, aides of 20 Across

54 Remove a beard
55 Rainbow goddess
56 Out of work
57 Exterior
58 Chablis or Chianti
59 Beaks
60 Employers
61 Freezes
62 Bothersome bug

DOWN

1 "Ah, me!"
2 TV series on Korean War medicos
3 Suits to __
4 Unpitying
5 Mississippi River discoverer
6 "Wonderland" girl
7 Arena for skaters
8 Versifier Ogden __
9 Farmer, at times
10 Rises from
11 Peak
12 Greek letters
13 Dictionary abbr.
21 Abate
22 Speechify
25 DeLuise role
26 Type of committee
27 Property claims
28 Foot-leg connector
29 Office need

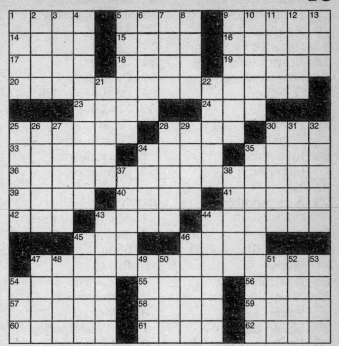

40

30 Gladden
31 Russian
revolutionary
32 Slain Egyptian
leader: 1981
34 Wound mark
35 Beclouding
37 Musical about Sra.
Perón
38 Mistrust
43 Potatoes and yams
44 Scottish maids

45 At no time
46 Threefold
47 In this manner
48 Abominate
49 New Zealand bird
50 __ the Red
51 Noted British
nobleman
52 Banishment isle
53 Try
54 Former French
coin

ACROSS

1 To a distance
5 Fragrance
10 Rosemary, e.g.
14 Come in second
15 Novarro of silents
16 Feat for Scott Hamilton
17 Vex
19 Here Hannibal was defeated
20 International merchant
21 Tap
23 A memorable Coward
24 Swindle
25 "An __ Rhapsody": Ward
28 A Caroline island
30 "The __ Reason": Paine
33 Music group
35 German playwright Hochhuth
37 Regret
38 "Off the Court" author
39 Jet set
41 Surfeit
42 Jazzman Winding
43 "__! poor Yorick": Hamlet
44 Like some cheese
46 Van Gogh painted here
48 Pos. opposite

50 Pitchers
51 A Roosevelt
53 Jacob's first wife
55 Tumult
57 __ box
61 Harvest
62 Clean fish
64 Commedia dell'__
65 Kind of pie
66 Location
67 Disinformed
68 Duck down
69 Animation

DOWN

1 Sheltered, at sea
2 Jimmie of diamond fame
3 P.D.Q.
4 Use a woofer
5 Alpine crest
6 Seldom
7 General Bradley
8 Pithy remark
9 "__ of robins . . .": Kilmer
10 Pledge's problem
11 Emulate Baron Munchausen
12 San __, on the Riviera
13 Sheep sound
18 Opposite of supine
22 Edith Giovanna Gassion
24 Primer pooch
25 Honshu city

82

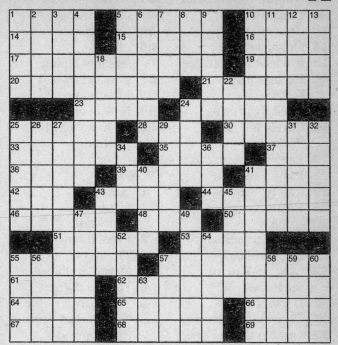

26 Composer Franck
27 Cheer
29 Go up
31 Exterior
32 Gratifies
34 Hill, in Arabic
36 Regatta unit
40 Alley
41 Carpenter's frame
43 Large land mass
45 "The Cloister and the Hearth" author

47 Married in haste
49 Ricochet
52 __ fraîche
54 Stage direction
55 River to the Caspian
56 First opera composer
57 Hang
58 Upbraid
59 "__ boy!"
60 Observed
63 Clock-dial number

ACROSS

1 "60 Minutes" co-host
6 Charitable gift
10 Jazz singing style
14 Cognizant
15 Ancient Persian foe
16 Do honors at
teatime
17 Most dignified
19 Coney Island's __
Park
20 Literary monogram
21 Put on the line
22 Six, for the big hand
24 Respect highly
26 Choice
28 Castle material?
30 Puts on hold
32 Largest African
antelope
35 Dormant
37 Crewman at Henley
39 Lincoln Center seat
40 Reduces, with
"down"
41 Pull up stakes
42 Glide at St. Moritz
43 La __ of Milano
44 Held a watch on
45 Not wholly
47 Predicament
49 Follows slavishly
51 "__, one vote"
55 Self-absorption
57 Feels poorly
59 Part of a royal flush

60 Pontifical name
61 Woo
64 Concerning
65 Otherwise
66 Miguel __
(Mickey Mouse)
67 Musical from a T. S.
Eliot book
68 New Look creator
69 Wide-spouted
pitchers

DOWN

1 "Le __ du
printemps":
Stravinsky
2 French-leave group
3 Victim of
Mephistopheles
4 Fall from grace
5 Tire with new life
6 "Lucky Jim" author
7 Scallions' kin
8 A.M.A. members
9 Pioneers
10 Edit film
11 Milieu for Darrow
12 Polly, to Tom Sawyer
13 Cafeteria utensil
18 Describe
23 Weigh by lifting
25 Anglo-Saxon slave
27 Swellings
29 Widen
31 Except
32 Overhead rail lines

84

42

33 Norse god of
mischief
34 Henry V won here:
Oct. 1415
36 Nothing
38 Roulette bet
40 Cut corners
41 Tiny arachnid
43 Weakens
44 Shaving of a
monk's head

46 Balances
48 Style of shirt
50 Authority
52 Not glossy
53 Greene or Sheen
54 Signs of our times
55 Long poem
56 Lollobrigida
58 Jack Frost?
62 __ Baba
63 Cold and damp

ACROSS

1 On the ball
6 Crease
10 Gable or Garbo
14 Gung-ho
15 Dramatic award
16 Wyandot's cousin
17 Geometric forms
19 Toff
20 Agent
21 Stun
22 Make uniform
24 Wordplay
25 Balanced
26 Gallery
29 Celestial blazer
30 Lusterless
33 Leather strip
34 Bridge master
35 __ Kabibble
36 Algonquian pole
37 All-purpose trk.
38 Oklahoma's Golden Hurricane
40 Formicary dweller
41 A.k.a. Barnaby Jones
43 Marital addition
44 Arikara
45 Knicks's rivals
46 State of equilibrium
47 "Midnight Cowboy" role
49 Word of woe
50 Put side by side
52 Apartment, e.g.
53 Python's kin
56 Den
57 Good dispatcher's activity
60 Shade
61 Pillar: Comb. form
62 Edwards or Lombardi
63 Cat that was born free
64 Suggestion
65 Wrote "30"

DOWN

1 Cliques
2 Lyra
3 ". . . I'm __ deceiver": G. Colman
4 Tie material
5 Forms of bigotry
6 Nerds
7 Sad news note
8 Topper
9 Warrant
10 Musical transition
11 Roads to nowhere
12 "__ We Got Fun?": 1921 song
13 Anagram for tree
18 District
23 Measurable
24 Door section
25 Marta of films
26 Rose oil

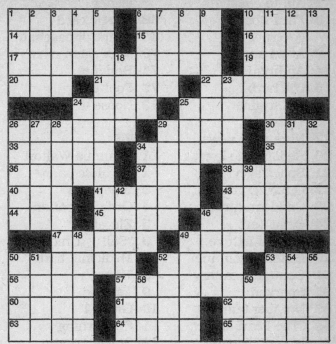

43

27 Swiss river
28 Split metal
fasteners
29 Students' jottings
31 Very, to Ozawa
32 Responds to
heat
34 Zest
39 Fingernails: Sp.
42 Implore
46 Glided
48 Trunk line

49 In re
50 Der __ (Adenauer)
51 Nursery-rhyme
vessel
52 Follower of
54 Down
53 Secure
54 Grimm opening
55 Antique
58 Reading on some
clocks
59 Stannum

ACROSS

1 Au, to chemists
5 First woman governor
9 At an angle
14 An Iroquoian
15 Dill herb
16 Entertainer Tucker
17 November news
20 Repairs the lawn
21 Space agcy.
22 U.S.N.A. grad
23 Caddoan Indian
24 Orbit part
26 Kind of lettuce
29 Dutch commune
31 Confine a canary
35 Sparked
37 Number suffix
40 "The Pearl of __ Island": Stowe
41 Political meeting
44 Greenland town
45 Stake
46 Type of orange
47 Earth tones
49 Sister
51 Draft initials
52 Bow or Barton
55 So, to Burns
57 Air: Abbr.
60 Tattle
61 Everglades birds
65 Declaration leader
68 Mystic card
69 Felipe of baseball
70 Norwegian river
71 Bouquet
72 Foot part
73 Noose

DOWN

1 Grandpa Walton
2 Heraldic band
3 Whoppers
4 Ornamentation
5 Elevated
6 "Sail __ Union . . . !"
7 Medicinal herb
8 Thong
9 Achieve
10 Greek T
11 Concerning
12 Singer Loretta
13 Russian news agency
18 Informal in taste
19 Ancient Jewish sect member
25 Ayr natives
26 Hatteras et al.
27 Declaim
28 Fight
30 Collar or jacket
32 Solos
33 Quaffs for tars

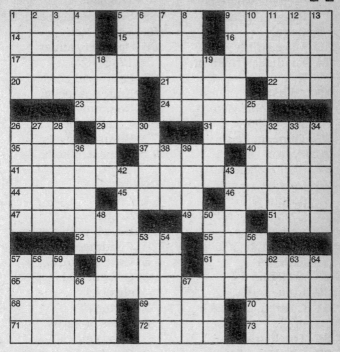

44

34 Serfs
36 Moral
38 Suffix with persist
39 Level
42 Memorable cellist
43 Youthful period
48 Type of German silver
50 Beneficial
53 Indian prince
54 White poplar

56 Flynn of films
57 "__ boy!"
58 "__ she blows!"
59 Hero of a Katz book
62 "__ Perpetua," Idaho motto
63 Corrida beast
64 Cinch
66 Pop's mate
67 Opponent

ACROSS

1 "Tell me where is fancy __": Shak.
5 Canal
10 Move swiftly
14 Footballer Tobin or Kyle
15 Adjust
16 Napoleonic victory site: 1796
17 Thine, in Tours
18 Type of eagle
19 Sheltered, at sea
20 Capone's political position?
22 Eyed cheesecake
23 An inert gas
24 Jack rabbit's long features
26 Antiquated
29 In the buff
31 Cleared, as profit
35 Truck driver
37 Greek markets
38 Biblical weed
39 Gypsy man
41 One margin of victory
42 Reveal
45 Separate
48 Give, as aid
49 Birthright seller
50 Dutch town
51 Water plant
53 Pleasant
55 Vote in
58 Confuse author Thomas?
63 Supermarket section
64 Singer Mel
65 Spanish painter: 1746-1828
66 Latin primer word
67 Knife sharpener
68 Columnist Shirley
69 "__ are called . . ."
70 Brain passages
71 Comedian Foxx

DOWN

1 Crow
2 Roster
3 British public school
4 Condescend
5 Have a quarrel
6 Ornamental tropical shrub
7 Portent
8 Glass or garter follower
9 Conger
10 Hail author Irving?
11 Droop
12 __ fixe
13 All even
21 Sties
22 Neighbor of Wash.
25 Collection of sayings
26 Mink's relative
27 G.I.'s holiday
28 Late singer Bobby
30 Eat away
32 Treasure __

90

45

33 Alleviated
34 Farm-equipment pioneer
36 Repair Chicago's slums?
40 Wrong-name error
43 Welshman, e.g.
44 Work unit
46 Certain ships or boats
47 "__ is life!"
52 Underway

54 Type of beaver
55 Dutch cheese
56 British Open golf winner: 1964
57 Zest
59 Writer Sarah __ Jewett
60 Took the el
61 Tinted
62 Stock enclosure
64 Sulfur: Comb. form

ACROSS

1 Shaded retreat
6 Obstacle
10 Sikorsky
14 __ firma
15 Goddess of youth
16 Exploding star
17 Writer Hammond __
18 Author Wister
19 Please
20 Calm
22 French department
23 She, in Paris
24 Dodged
26 Objects
30 Global area, in poesy
32 Immediately
33 Kan. city
35 Wall recess
39 Expanded
41 Underwater fisherman
43 Saying
44 Famous Italian family
46 Approaching
47 Motionless
49 Late bloomers
51 Box
54 Verb suffix
56 Samoan seaport
57 Calm
63 Fourth-down play
64 Hence
65 Motherless calf
66 Gaelic
67 Yemeni seaport
68 Fla. city
69 Marshy plant
70 G.O.P. leader
71 Garment inserts

DOWN

1 Suffix with system
2 Las Vegas rival
3 City SE of Prague
4 Pitcher Hershiser
5 Bacon slice
6 Sandbar
7 F.D.R. shibboleth
8 Have __ in one's bonnet
9 Masculine, e.g.
10 Calm
11 Small-necked bottle
12 Like sheep
13 Appraised
21 Actress Janis
25 Queue
26 Art style
27 Okla. city
28 Ocean sunfish
29 Calm

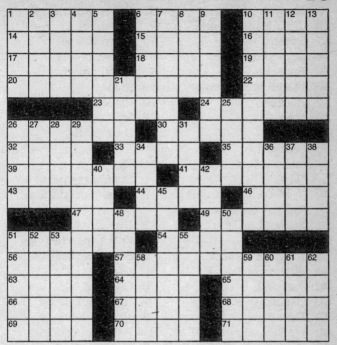

46

31 Speedy
34 Frankfurt's river
36 Mont. Indian
37 Listen to
38 Slips
40 Sinew: Comb. form
42 __ Melba
45 Baseball's Casey
48 Group of nine
50 Mariner

51 Frisk
52 Venezuelan river
53 Wash cycle
55 Type of pastry
58 Catholic booklet
59 Off one's rocker
60 Jelly thickener
61 African river
62 Cambric and oolong

ACROSS

1 First fratricide
5 Musical family
10 Japanese religious center
14 Actress Sommer
15 Apportion
16 Victim of 1 Across
17 Reclines
18 Free
19 Fervor
20 Leonardo masterpiece, with "The"
22 __ Moro, memorable Italian statesman
23 Some M.I.T. grads
24 __ Diego
25 Offshore hazard
26 Written order
30 Parched
32 Expert
33 Telescope part
35 Wed
39 Genesis place
43 Meuse River city
44 Word with fatted or golden
45 Break a fast
46 A homophone for meat
49 Newspaper V.I.P.'s
51 Rio Muni seaport
54 They, in Tours
56 West of Hollywood
57 Russian lake
58 Occupants of 39 Across
63 Fire: Comb. form
64 Furnish a new crew
65 Christian and Abraham
66 Third Gospel
67 Biblical lyres
68 Fixed amount
69 Signet
70 Plant support
71 Wall word: Dan. 5:25

DOWN

1 Monastery part
2 Former Jordanian queen
3 D.D.E.'s namesakes
4 Fitted together
5 Staircase railing part
6 Crooked
7 Hoof sounds
8 Namesakes of a Hebrew prophet
9 Tristram Shandy's creator
10 Asch's "The __"
11 White poplar
12 Peg Woffington's creator
13 __ a sudden (unexpectedly)
21 Liner's path
26 Tatamis
27 Yearn
28 Want
29 Finis
31 Hoodlum

94

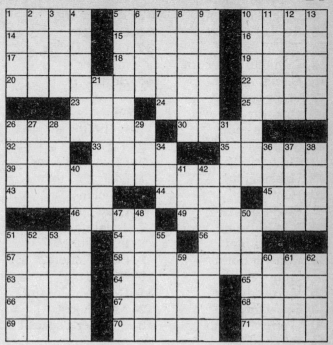

34 Dry, as wine
36 Idea: Comb. form
37 Rent
38 Tolkien creatures
40 Teacher of Saul of
Tarsus: Acts 22:3
41 Scottish negative
42 "Mosses from an __":
Hawthorne
47 Coronets
48 Adjective for
1 Across

50 Hymn of praise
to God
51 Scoops
52 Dispute
53 Japanese
poem
55 Islands north of
Tonga
59 Second Gospel
60 Seabird
61 Peacockish
62 Ferrara name

ACROSS

1 Copy, for short
5 Glacial leftover
10 Kind of concert
14 Jason's ship
15 Criminal's concern
16 Director Kazan
17 Shaw opus
20 One way to travel
21 Golfer's coup
22 Some
23 Celt
25 Unassuming
29 Homer or Shakespeare
30 E.M.K. is one
33 Wading bird
34 Conspiratorial group
35 Vein contents
36 Shaw opus
40 "Perfect" number
41 Witch of __
42 Wagnerian goddess
43 Compass pt.
44 Creditor's claim
45 Maiden
47 N.Y. heroes in 1986
48 A rel.
49 Poetic placement
52 Cake date
57 Shaw opus
60 Viscount's superior
61 High-climbing vine
62 Theater org.
63 Sea eagle
64 Golden Horde member
65 Bring up

DOWN

1 Pronounces
2 Jog
3 Chills and fever
4 Dial __
5 Scholar
6 Gray poem
7 To laugh, in Lyon
8 First letters
9 Secret letters?
10 Flower part
11 Designer Cassini
12 Aspirin, e.g.
13 Shopper's special
18 Ages
19 Tailor's tool
23 Eva or Magda
24 OPEC member
25 Catchers' necessities
26 Woodwind instruments
27 A consort of Zeus
28 Superlative suffix
29 Stick for Ozawa
30 Entrances
31 Wear

48

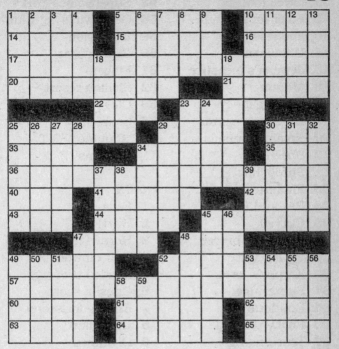

32 Decoration for a G.I.
34 Surrenders
37 Soften
38 Entity
39 Jewel
45 Less bright
46 Anon., e.g.
47 Actress Oberon
48 Artemis, to a Roman

49 Quaker word
50 Have on
51 Merit
52 Licked
53 White frost
54 Cape Cod hill
55 Charles's pooch
56 Timespan
58 Short-order order
59 Creek

ACROSS

1 Dwell (on)
5 Fiber for rope
10 Footless
14 U.S. satellite
15 Jeweler's measure
16 Mummer
17 Passing fancy
18 Like Poe's poems
20 Roman councils
22 Sheen, in Shropshire
23 Pindarics
24 Rex and Donna
26 Curved
28 Shoot the breeze
29 "__ la Douce"
33 Karpov's forte
34 Subterfuge
35 Boutique
36 Rocky pinnacle
37 Trucking rigs
38 Actress Claire
39 Essence
41 "Oh, __ in England . . .": Browning
42 He was Lou Grant
44 Level, in Lincolnshire
45 Winglike
46 Butler of fiction
47 Railroad tracks
49 __ ex machina

50 Bellhop's mission
53 SuperSonics' turf
56 Gershwin's "__ Blue"
59 Excursion
60 Grid figures
61 Fingers
62 Sicilian resort
63 Cloy
64 Soap chip
65 "Camino __": T. Williams

DOWN

1 Fells
2 Hurt
3 Horned mammal
4 Hair ointments
5 Landed property
6 Cries of scorn
7 Ending for secret
8 Grimalkin
9 Olympics contestants
10 "__ as good as a mile"
11 Scot's ancient associate
12 Baseball's Moreno
13 Stet's opposite
19 Goner's name
21 Spreads to dry
24 Hispanic dances: Var.
25 Less strenuous

26 Equity member
27 Sitcom of the 70's
28 Cooked with a spicy sauce
30 Imitation diamond
31 French Impressionist
32 Divorced
37 Tie
40 Backslide
42 Terrain
43 Camera part
48 Office-holders
49 Compact
50 Makes a wrong turn
51 Flightless bird
52 George of films
53 Word with screen or stocking
54 Kind of moth
55 Of a period
57 __ City, Okla.
58 Affirmative vote

ACROSS

1 Open somewhat
5 Twinklers
10 Pequod's skipper
14 No great shakes
15 Martinique peak
16 Pram pusher
17 First change to 35 Across
20 Memorabilia
21 Count calories
22 Bribe
23 Ditty
24 Chicago gridder
25 Actress McDaniel
28 Verve
29 Sch.-zone sign
32 Bitter
33 Briefed
34 Manifestation
35 Masterpiece of 1787
38 Wales's floral emblem
39 Corrida kudos
40 T.L.C. maven
41 Strange
42 Say it is so
43 Squabble
44 Chafe
45 Baseball's Connie
46 Warning of yore
49 Bit of ice
50 Song introduced in "Sunny"
53 Day to celebrate 17 Across
56 Roy's wife
57 Raise the spirits
58 Extremely
59 Pitcher Chandler
60 Unbending
61 Summit

DOWN

1 Nick and Nora's pooch
2 A Barrymore
3 On the Aegean
4 Burgle
5 Carpentry groove
6 Part of AT&T
7 Heaps
8 Ump's cousin
9 "__ York," 1941 movie
10 Wrath
11 Guffaw
12 Certain colonists
13 Diamond feature
18 A Broadway hit: 1966
19 Ex-shahdom
23 Cudgel
24 City on the Loire
25 Creator of "Little Iodine"
26 Throbbed
27 At bay
28 Inscribe

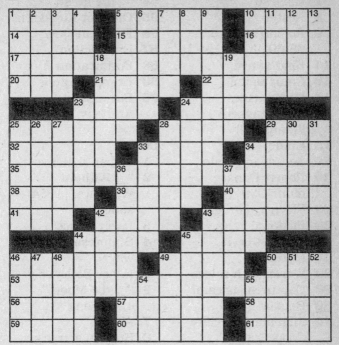

29	Goldbrick	44	Unbound
30	At large	45	Civilian wear
31	Person of property	46	Amplifies
33	Key	47	Vault
34	Adhered	48	Rights org.
36	Election time	49	Rugged rock
37	Halloween	50	Cry
	beneficiary	51	On earth
42	Cuckoopint	52	Gemstone
43	Handled tenderly;	54	Inventor Whitney
	humored	55	U.S. dam complex

ACROSS

1 Enclose
5 Roster
9 Roman emperor: 68-69
14 Kind of test
15 Court name
16 Mishmashes
17 __ me tangere (hands off!)
18 Erode
19 Setting for "Rain"
20 Robert Donat film: 1939
23 Electrical unit
24 Fictional Jane
25 Novelist Levin
27 Maroon
32 Woven with ridges
36 Captures, as game
39 Bender
40 Film starring Gary Cooper: 1932
43 Moslem magistrate
44 Toward shelter, at sea
45 Accordion part
46 Meredith's "The __ of Richard Feverel"
48 Finial
50 Advantage
53 State of lawlessness
58 Dreyfuss-Mason film: 1977
62 Small cabaret
63 Money in Milan
64 __ the finish
65 Omni or Kingdome
66 Freeman's "R. __"
67 Interdiction
68 Fortification
69 European gulls
70 Barbara or Anthony

DOWN

1 Cuban dance
2 "__ Without Windows," 1964 song
3 Lively dance
4 Suppress, in a way
5 F. Lee Bailey, e.g.
6 "__ the Moon," 1953 song
7 Abash
8 English actress: 1847-1928
9 Land of plenty
10 Jai __
11 Flaccid
12 Bronx cheers
13 __ rule (generally)
21 "The Bartered __"
22 Arête
26 Fourth person
28 Cit. of Padua
29 Dry
30 Tibetan monk
31 Once, once

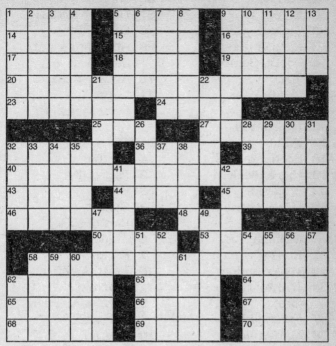

32	City on the Brazos
33	Out yonder
34	Star of "Shane"
35	Lake or canal
37	October potable
38	Kind of club
41	Ralph __ Emerson
42	Deem
47	Sea between Greece and Turkey
49	Earners
51	Jewish folklore figure
52	Roman official
54	Pointed arch
55	Dug for coal
56	Incensed
57	Singer John
58	Sped
59	Sped
60	Volcano in Sicily
61	Concoct
62	Estop

ACROSS

1 Portico
5 Defeat
9 Skillful
13 Mets or Jets
14 Tooth: Comb. form
15 Needle case
16 Actress Lanchester
17 Fund
18 Scotland __
19 Has a drink
22 __ Lanka
23 Dry, as wine
24 Some coll. linemen
27 Russia's Sea of __
30 Tower builder
35 Within: Comb. form
37 Emerald Isle
39 Marketplace
40 Crow or boast
43 Vacant
44 Lid adjunct
45 Thought
46 __ up (bungles)
48 __ over (reenlist)
50 Coll. org. in the 60's
51 Ethiopian prince
53 Units in the yr.
55 Pushes one's products
64 List of duties
65 Be a pest
66 Jot
67 Dec. 24 and 31
68 Savor
69 New York's state flower
70 Author Rebecca __
71 Deps.
72 Perceive as fact

DOWN

1 Seethe
2 Part of TV
3 Kiln
4 Collect
5 Part of N.B.
6 At loose __
7 Packs
8 North American sparrow
9 Former Algerian V.I.P.'s
10 Coup d'__
11 Roll up
12 Flood or spring
14 Dweller
20 A feast __ famine
21 Suffix with tact
24 Desert shrub
25 Dwarf
26 Discontinues
28 Russian city
29 Passes
31 E-J connection
32 Some are frozen
33 Was wrong

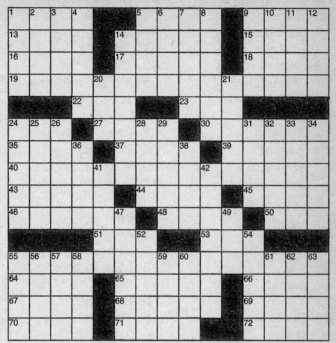

34 Turner and Cantrell
36 Mel and Ed of baseball
38 Munch on
41 Legal copies
42 Fanciful notion
47 Fries quickly
49 Hawaiian dish
52 Exhausted
54 "The Hunting of the __": Carroll

55 Barrymore or Pearson
56 Wander
57 Salt Lake City team
58 Topgallant
59 __ California
60 Service centers for G.I.'s
61 Town near London
62 Middling
63 European duck

ACROSS

1 Taj Mahal site
5 Humane org.
9 Dutch painter Frans
13 French soldier
15 Corrida cries
16 Biblical twin
17 Celebrities
19 Assistant
20 Jargon
21 Midnight's antithesis
23 "The King __"
25 Agt.
26 Eskimo's "giddyap!"
30 Alley __ of comics
31 Titter sound
34 Suffix with resist
35 Kind of squad
37 White cliffs spot
39 Thought
40 Come in
42 Roman fiddler
43 Gives temporarily
45 Autry or Tunney
46 Arthurian lady
47 Lease anew
49 Indicate approval
50 Fr. holy women
51 __ Jima

52 Snare
54 Gentlemen of Verona
57 Mob
61 Pshaw!
62 Tête-à-tête
65 Aid an arsonist
66 The Oder, to a Czech
67 Pony or bean
68 Employs
69 Santa's largess
70 Pindar's output

DOWN

1 Away from: Prefix
2 Departs
3 Iranian coin
4 Star of "M*A*S*H"
5 Heir, often
6 Delegate with full power
7 Food fish
8 Classify
9 Hearing devices
10 Land mass
11 Astor was one
12 Sunbonnet girl
14 Forearm bone
18 Disregard
22 Require
24 Up and __
26 Post
27 Below

28 Play part
29 Auto's "eyes"
32 Occasion
33 Weird
36 Quartet member
38 Heaters
41 Edit
44 Stitched
48 "__ to Handle,"
   1938 film
53 Set piece

54 Part-time tchrs.
55 What "video"
   means
56 Change décor
58 Paducah's river
59 Make one's
   way
60 Calendar item
61 Greek letter
63 "__ Rheingold"
64 Author __ Passos

ACROSS

1 Weskit
5 Ambassador's asset
9 Cheap tire
14 Straight: Comb. form
15 Part of "Oyez!"
16 Part of a Stein line
17 Dies __
18 Writer __ Bombeck
19 Special talent
20 Abundance
23 Cookie
24 The bull, in Barcelona
25 Massenet opera
27 Singer Yma __
30 Incite
33 Far East staple
36 Nigerian natives
38 Point of view
39 Foofaraw
40 What tight shoes cause
42 "All well," in space
43 Certain Slavs
46 Module
47 Work measures
48 Some British kings
50 Ieper, to the French
52 Chair or car
54 Intemperance
58 Sunken fence
60 Pudding ingredient
63 Chew the scenery
65 Competes
66 Belém's river
67 Arabian coffee
68 To be, to Bernadette
69 Kin of etc.
70 Printer's roller
71 "Shane" star
72 Geodesic __

DOWN

1 The __ (Sinatra)
2 Flynn of filmdom
3 "Gentlemen, __ your engines"
4 On __ (precisely)
5 "The perception of __ is a tie of sympathy . . .": Emerson
6 Plane preceder
7 David is one
8 Characteristic
9 British mil. group
10 Soil problem
11 A dextrose
12 The Charles's pet
13 Kind of hole
21 S.A. country
22 Eureka!
26 Altar in the sky
28 __ Ben Adhem

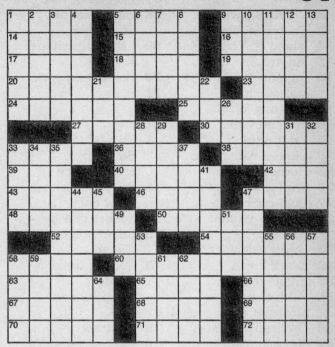

54

29 Like this puzzle?
31 Walk through mud
32 Sounds a mouse evokes
33 Impetuous
34 __ fixe
35 Stack of stalks
37 Sassy lass
41 Accented
44 Inhale
45 A Chaplin
47 Houdini did it

49 Bursa
51 Annex or ell: Abbr.
53 New
55 Poetry Muse
56 Vamoose!
57 An oil source
58 Half: Prefix
59 Egyptian deity
61 Actress Moreno
62 Twerp's cousin
64 Iowa farm item

ACROSS

1 Flavor
6 Caesar's partner
10 Snatch suddenly
14 Island off Venezuela
15 Mil. truant
16 Ingredient in succotash
17 Henning forte
18 Punch-in time
19 Fruit drinks
20 Subordinate player
23 Horned viper
26 Canine problem
27 Cold-cut counters
28 Twain's original surname
30 Burns's denial
32 Break bread
33 Edible rootstock
34 Faith of the Moslems
36 Orchestra member
42 "George White's Scandals," e.g.
43 Kind of chamber
45 Inside dope
48 First follower
49 Tutor of Héloïse
52 Store
54 De Valera
56 Mire
57 Part of a parade
60 Woody's son
61 Coarsely ground pulse
62 Down source

66 Mexican city
67 Laborer of yore
68 Birthplace of St. Teresa
69 Peut-__ (perhaps): Fr.
70 Boris of Bulgaria
71 Resign

DOWN

1 TV's "My Sister __"
2 Southern constellation
3 Small dog with a curly tail
4 Sashes in Nara
5 Inflorescence on a stem
6 Contrapuntal musical compositions
7 Due
8 Contract
9 Hebrew letter: Var.
10 Area in the woods
11 What Oedipus solved
12 Pilot Earhart
13 Most lowdown
21 Put up
22 Beau __
23 Pretend
24 Pole, for one
25 Lovely girl
29 Othello, e.g.
31 Entire
34 Diamonds, to a hood

110

35 Honey: Sp.
37 Set of three hounds, in hunting
38 Egg: Comb. form
39 State of undress
40 Con man's ruse
41 By means of, for short
44 Eccentric
45 Treat in Taxco
46 Turkish hospice
47 Beauty __

49 "Journey Into Fear" author
50 Neckpiece
51 Group of nine
53 Tidbit for tea
55 Capital of Guam
58 "__ a man . . ."
59 Emulate Phil Boggs
63 Switch to low beam
64 Actor Wallach
65 Ship's deserter

ACROSS

1 Captain's boat
4 Poplar
9 Robber
14 Mo. in spring
15 Wanderer
16 Swarm
17 Classic preceder
18 __-Rivieres, city in Canada
19 Red or reddish
20 Old French coin
21 Faneuil __, Boston
22 Put duds on
23 Bundle of bound sticks
25 Norton's adit
29 Room in an abbey
30 Cambodian coin
31 Carton
32 English cathedral city
34 Actress Claire
35 Yorkshire river
36 Missus, in 68 Across
41 Complete
42 Ottoman V.I.P.
43 Final fig.
44 Silkworm
45 Hugh Capet was one
46 Nine-banded armadillo
49 Moving against the current
52 Bartender's device
55 Sigmoid letter
56 Shoot the breeze
57 Pay dirt
58 Righteous
61 Tine
62 Family
63 Suburb of Brussels
64 Item in a makeup kit
65 Foot width
66 Wind-blown soil
67 Chose
68 Aust. state

DOWN

1 Rascal
2 S.A. shrub
3 Outstanding, in 68 Across
4 Formic mounds
5 Navigational aid
6 Soap plant
7 Armor
8 __ bodkins
9 O.T. book
10 Turbulent, as seas
11 Fort __, Calif.
12 Strange
13 Of crucial importance
22 Former Japanese P.M.
24 Golfer's number 4 wood
25 Reform
26 Sashes in Soka
27 Savant's acquisition

112

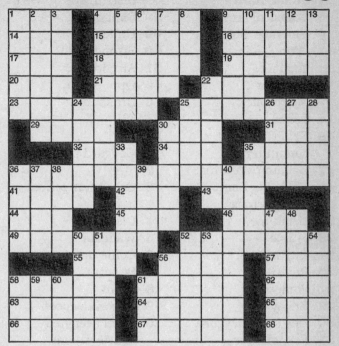

28 Unknowns, in
   algebra
30 Peninsula in NE
   Egypt
33 Longs
35 Fall flower
36 Algonquian language
37 Difficult
38 Wife of Geraint
39 Hyped up
40 Encroached
47 Shattered

48 High homes
50 Time periods
51 Man and Wight
52 Treat to drinks, in
   68 Across
53 Color slightly
54 Take up again
56 Bird's pouch
58 Singer Tormé
59 Ab __ (from the start)
60 Dakotan Indian
61 Expert

ACROSS

1 Finish third
5 Classical lang.
8 Calendar abbr.
11 "For __ jolly good . . ."
12 Inventor McCormick
14 Portal
15 Semirural commuter
17 Grimm beginning
18 Phil's Pa. home in re 49 Across
20 "Ulalume" writer
23 __ fixe
24 City in N.H.
25 Registers
27 Pompous
29 Envoy
30 Doe or Barleycorn
31 Fox follower
32 Bea Arthur TV role
34 Small bottle
38 Back talk
39 Rare
41 Sockeye, e.g.
45 Speaking masters
46 __ Gay, famed plane
47 Equipment
48 Society page word
49 February 2
53 Courageous
54 Otologist's instrument
58 Simians
59 Underneath
60 Strong wind
61 Airport info
62 Opp. of ant.
63 Brash talk

DOWN

1 Haggard heroine
2 Jinx
3 Columbus school letters
4 Distort
5 Wildcats
6 Come up
7 Ballerina's skirt
8 Poem
9 Cenozoic epoch
10 __ on (weighed heavily upon)
12 February 2
13 Tennis unit
14 Peg
16 Manufactured
19 Related
20 Skin
21 Unique person
22 Therefore
26 Cereal grain
27 Turf
28 Lamont Cranston's secret identity

114

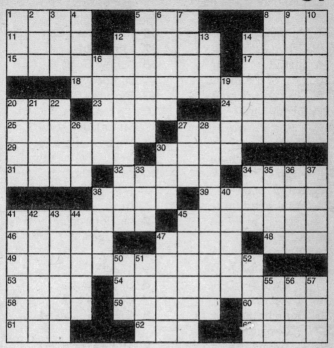

30 Au __ (menu term)
33 Wood for skis
34 Cask
35 Golf-bag item
36 Farm measure
37 __ majesté
38 Shensi capital
40 One of the Moluccas
41 Jamaican music form

42 Transported
43 Ill-fated
44 Chimney passages
45 Area
47 Devout
50 Stroke lightly
51 Tints
52 Safecracker
55 Greek letter
56 Sprite
57 Ump's cousin

ACROSS

1 Longfellow's "The Bell of __"
5 __ Ma Kettle
10 Secondhand
14 Install
15 One of the media
16 Drummer's goal
17 Diving bird
19 Indigo shrub
20 Resins
21 Business school subj.
23 E.T.O. boss
24 Point of a fountain pen
26 Edited
28 Idol's perch
33 Lead-in for graph or gram
34 "Drop me __"
35 Borscht base
37 __ Canyon Dam
40 Lampshade wearer
41 Dull finish
42 "I cannot tell __"
43 Poker pot part
44 In __ (bogged down)
45 __ down (intimidate)
46 Twisted hemp
48 Harried
50 Foxboro player
53 __ Miguel, Azores
54 Airline abbr.
55 Arabic letter
57 Fold

62 Astronaut Armstrong
64 Bulldozer
66 Freshwater fish
67 Threefold
68 "Show Boat" composer
69 Inquires
70 "__ Home," McCartney song
71 Partner of crafts

DOWN

1 ". . . __ forgive those . . ."
2 Duck or color
3 Charge
4 Entry
5 Toast
6 Sports org.
7 Roofer's tool
8 Caroline, to Ted Kennedy
9 Mineral or word with Alps
10 U.N. member
11 Sea urchin
12 Pass over
13 Struck out
18 Wash, in a way
22 Actor Sparks
25 Mogul dynasty founder
27 Make ineffective
28 Spotted cavy
29 Ardor
30 This isn't cricket!

116

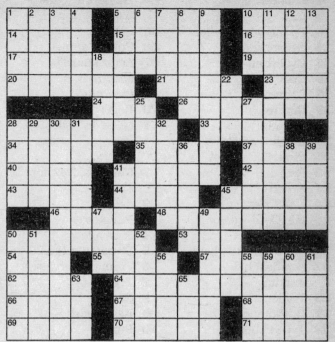

31 Make beloved
32 Pause
36 Diminutive suffixes
38 Ireland
39 Require
41 Famed matador: 1917-47
45 Signal or trooper preceder
47 Estuary
49 Kind of powder
50 Asian carnivore

51 Sectors
52 Three-tiered coronet
56 Glassmaker's ingredient
58 Greek Cypriot org.
59 Affirm
60 Painter José Maria __
61 Coastal fliers
63 "__ Misérables"
65 An explosive: Abbr.

ACROSS

1 London gallery
5 Ipso __
10 Spanish Surrealist
14 Actor Ladd
15 Gruesome
16 Russian river
17 __ avis
18 Revere
19 "Auntie __"
20 Discard smoking material?
22 Receded
23 Record
24 Him follower
26 N.Y.C.-to-Boston dir.
29 __ an ear (hearken)
31 Avoids a big wedding
35 Trade
37 Of the nerves
38 Type of bean
39 Comic-strip cry
41 Ibsen heroine
42 Roman amphitheaters
45 On the decline
48 Cousin of a leash
49 Signs showing success
50 Eds. receive them
51 Precinct
53 Aware of
55 Office worker
58 Regret of a reformed thief?

63 Garnish
64 "We're off __ the Wizard"
65 Privy to
66 College subj.
67 Actor Maurice
68 Miss Kett
69 Quantity
70 Belief
71 Glide on high

DOWN

1 Canvas cover, for short
2 Jai __
3 Pungent
4 Pass a law
5 Swinger in the 20's
6 Formal interview
7 Trim
8 Bores
9 Keats work
10 Puzzle
11 Yemeni, for one
12 Type of excuse
13 "__ Three Lives": Philbrick
21 Hearty's companion
22 Pronoun for a Parisienne
25 Dusk's time, to Tennyson
26 Brilliance
27 Black, in Boulogne
28 Irish patriot
30 Some sale documents

118

32 Introductory
remarks
33 Merits
34 Louvers
36 Clue to homo
sapiens?
40 Flammable oil
43 Plane or space
preceder
44 Before, poetically
46 Oppose
47 Movie dog

52 Get __ on (stir)
54 Migrant workers of
the 30's
55 Eskimo vehicle
56 Mexican staple
57 A god of love
59 "No man __ island":
Donne
60 Division word
61 __ bene
62 Growl
64 Asian holiday

ACROSS

1 Whittle
6 Proper
10 Sonny of Congress
14 Spikes the punch
15 Mystique
16 Mothers of lambs
17 Upset the boat
19 Crossword wild ox
20 Leaving a valid will
21 Usher's job
23 Brain passages
25 Danish city
26 Olympic trio
29 Material for a highway
31 Hayworth and Moreno
32 Plebe, e.g.
33 Cry of disgust
36 Hero
37 Type of race horse
38 Nimble
39 Enclose
40 Sea eagles
41 Clown
42 Make beloved
44 Palpitates
45 Pepys or Butler
47 Ladle
49 Invade
51 Pertains
55 Cribs
56 Degradation
58 Town SW of Padua
59 He was: Lat.
60 Gaucho's lasso
61 Movie maker Hunter
62 Resentful
63 Resource

DOWN

1 Keyhole
2 Possess
3 High cards
4 Opposite of horizontal
5 Manors, e.g.
6 Kitchen utensil
7 __ of the mill
8 Infuriates
9 Renovated
10 Defeated
11 Confessing
12 City lights
13 Okla. tribe
18 All purpose vehs.
22 Miner's access
24 Parts of typewriters
26 Handhold
27 Jockey
28 Reparations

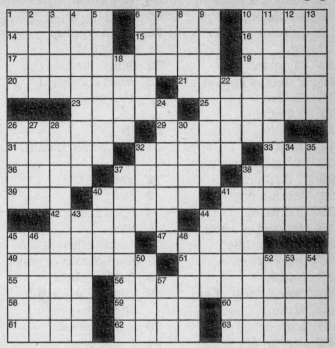

60

30 Fruity quaffs
32 Biblical town
34 Uproot
35 Pts. of triangles
37 Overtures
38 Cognomens
40 German reservoir dam
41 Deadly disease
43 Ministers to
44 "Tootsies"

45 Staid or subdued
46 Dispatch boat
48 Babble
50 Infamous fiddler
52 Receptions
53 Being, in Barcelona
54 Immediately, to a pharmacist
57 Tavern

ACROSS

1 Victor's reward
5 School orgs.
9 Collie or poodle, e.g.
14 Lily plant
15 Walesa of Poland
16 Bizarre
17 Uprising
18 Pa. city
19 Disposed
20 Maugham book
23 __ de plume
24 Pan-Am org.
25 Competed
27 Hit song of 1939
35 Eggs, to Cato
36 Unicorn fish
37 Tangle
38 Twerp's next of kin
40 Nettle
43 Jog
44 Certain Art Deco works
46 School book
48 Numero __
49 Song from "The New Moon": 1928
53 Kind of fur
54 Genetic inits.
55 Scot's precipitation
58 Diabolical concoction
64 Kind of lily
66 Hebrew eternity
67 Part of N.B.
68 To have: Fr.
69 Level
70 Asian country
71 Classified
72 Is indebted
73 Word combined with while

DOWN

1 French recreation spot
2 Inter __
3 Stare
4 Bolide
5 Nice
6 Aquatic flier
7 Kind of rain or test
8 Gather wheat
9 Some masquerade attendees
10 Capek classic
11 Collar type
12 Rubik or Rapee
13 Judge
21 Movies' "Elephant Boy"
22 Diamond __
26 No-no word
27 Archaeologists' finds
28 Turn outward
29 Have an __ the ground
30 Certain grass

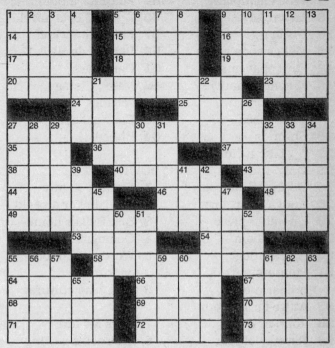

31 Ranch in "Giant"
32 Alarm, old style
33 Norse coin
34 Ill. city
39 __ ex machina
41 Sunday talk: Abbr.
42 Go to __ (overdo)
45 Club or ship employee
47 Hamilton bills
50 "Bali __"

51 Corrida figure
52 Putter
55 Shoo
56 Shade of blue
57 Leaning
59 Kind of hammer
60 Weather word
61 Bring up
62 Slaughter of baseball
63 Bridge seat
65 Golfer's concern

ACROSS

1 True Olympian
8 Advertise
15 Discharge
16 Makes soda water
17 First spaceman
18 Penzance natives?
19 Points on compasses
20 Shrouds
22 "__ Like It Hot"
23 Only, in Bonn
24 Dep's. counterpart
25 Andy Gump's wife
26 Chamber piece
28 Blois bloom
30 "Great" dog
31 Painters' preparations
33 Attire for Lamour
35 John or Jane
36 Reverse of rear
37 Monte Carlo attractions
41 Orwell or Saki, e.g.
45 Amor's wings
46 Comes closer
48 Wise __ owl
49 Small ape
50 Gram or center starter
51 Where Mao ruled: Abbr.

52 Arabia's Gulf of __
54 Place for a bout
56 "__ 18," Uris novel
57 Face the kickoff
59 Sahara dweller: Var.
61 Conceives
62 Mise __ (stage setting)
63 Easy gallops
64 Ebbed

DOWN

1 Shades of gray
2 A bushel or a peck
3 Ben Bella's home
4 Oolong and hyson
5 Word with phone or trumpet
6 Overseas cultural org.
7 Cars for hire
8 Pharaoh's writing material
9 Old Brazilian currency
10 Boston Bruins' Bobby
11 Pastoral sounds
12 Imperial seat?
13 Raining cats and dogs
14 Ancient ascetics
21 Plural of is
27 D.J.'s golden __

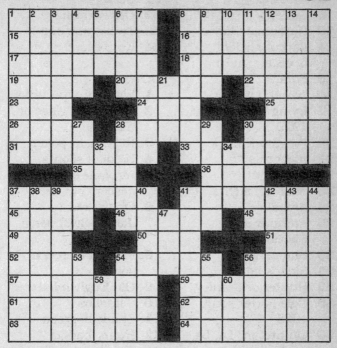

28 Freezer coolant
29 S.R.O. causers
30 Singer Summer
32 Ages upon ages
34 Showed one's heels
37 Pertaining to heat
38 Walk among the trees
39 Crusader's foe
40 Feminine foreteller

41 Computer adjunct
42 Had high hopes
43 Actress Dietrich
44 In custody
47 Mimic
53 Straight
54 State confidently
55 Tops
56 Defense against a mugger
58 Mennon ending
60 U.C.L.A. rival

ACROSS

1 U.N.'s U __
6 Suffer
10 Rumanian dance
14 Part of ancient Greece
15 Foray
16 "When I was __ . . ."
17 Irving Berlin song: 1929
20 Pragmatic ones
21 River quay
22 Shoot out
23 Saharan sights
24 Arose
28 Anthony and Clarissa
30 Shiraz native
31 Skier's lift
32 Hunter or Stanley
35 Cole Porter song: 1935
39 Quintet in "La, La, Lucille"
40 N.F.L. employees
41 Imam's faith
42 Asparagus stalk
44 Compact
45 Delights
48 Teed off
51 The British call this asdic
52 Most substantial
56 Freed-Brown song: 1929
59 Pa. city

60 Word with shoppe
61 Beam
62 Desideratum
63 Tweed was one
64 Keep score

DOWN

1 Waiter's expectation
2 Word with glass or hand
3 Kick in, in poker
4 Naldi of silents
5 Airplane's swift descent
6 Originated
7 James-Swift song: 1929
8 Most of Mercer's songs
9 Old English letter
10 Seraglios
11 Shade of green
12 Honey badger
13 Woodworkers' tools
18 Tuck's companion
19 Gusto
23 Part of a parrot's beak
24 Scoff
25 City on the Oka
26 Aglets
27 Prefix with form or sex
29 Pecks at
31 "Take __ Train"
32 Ceramist's need

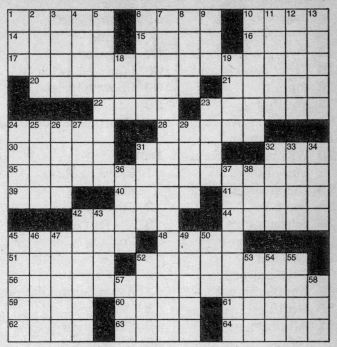

63

33 Actresses Claire and Balin
34 Same, in Somme
36 __ bien
37 Most frivolous
38 Take advantage of
42 Produced for public viewing
43 Lovely woman
45 City near Düsseldorf
46 France's longest river

47 Sharpshooter Oakley
49 Upbraids
50 Biblical verb ending
52 Venus de __
53 Writer Bombeck
54 Lateen or mizzen
55 Money compartment
57 Head: Slang
58 French marshal under Napoleon

ACROSS

1 Greek letters
5 "For Pete's __!"
9 Type of beam
14 Mascara recipient
15 Front of a caravel
16 Pippin
17 Youth org.
18 Land measure
19 Kingdom
20 Withhold corporal punishment
23 Defendants, in law
24 Peak
25 Slithery one
26 Lincoln's coin
27 Golf norm
30 Urge onward
32 Imprisonment
38 Heath
41 Absolute, as legal rights
43 Beseeches
44 Camel's problem
45 __ ha-Shanah
47 Garland at a luau
48 Town in Germany
50 Choose
53 Swing around
57 Asian holiday
58 Pocket money
62 Frankie or Cleo of songdom
64 Soft drink
65 Poster
66 Robin Hood's missile
67 Litigates
68 Like __ of bricks
69 Snow vehicles
70 Volcano in Sicily
71 Chanteuse Horne

DOWN

1 Cities in Minn. and Nev.
2 Fla. city
3 Tin Pan Alley org.
4 Portion
5 Tiff
6 __ of Titus
7 Asian peninsula
8 Pitchers
9 Fat from hogs
10 Gibbon, e.g.
11 Dinner item
12 Actress Terry
13 Mail a check
21 Fast train
22 Jupiter's mother
26 Oddity
28 __ in Able
29 Wealthy
31 Fretful
32 Tear
33 Monogram of "All Quiet . . ." author

64

34 Trunk item
35 Author of "The Other"
36 New Deal org.
37 Do farming
39 Ovid's 151
40 Loser to D.D.E.
42 __ à la mode
46 School dance
48 Book of maps
49 Singer Bailey

51 Outmoded
52 Game fish
54 Mountain group in Utah
55 Fuse
56 Incite
58 Stitches
59 Paradise
60 Spanish house
61 Sicilian resort
63 Become drowsy

ACROSS

1 Basic things
5 British pokey
9 Noncom
12 Actor Calhoun
13 Roman courts
15 Hun leader
16 Act to impress
18 This may be proper
19 Income's opposite
20 British princess
21 Angel, in Paris
22 Be mistaken
24 "Do not go __ . . .":
   D. Thomas
26 Small untruth
29 Sacred composition
31 Spats
33 Black cuckoo
34 __ Vegas
35 Papal envoy
37 Small sailing ship
40 Bothered
41 Invests
42 __ capita
43 Journey unit
44 Norse poem
45 About
47 Shakespearean sot
48 Houston team
50 Dress edge
52 Er __ (he says): Ger.
54 After: Prefix
56 Marx Brothers'
   "A Day at the __"

60 "Picnic" playwright
61 Holds a second job
63 Told a 26 Across
64 Metal mixture
65 Castle defense
66 Ancient
67 Anglo-Saxon
   laborer
68 Cobblers' tools

DOWN

1 Jason's ship
2 Brian __, a king of
   Ireland
3 Auto, Dixie or demo
   follower
4 Irish playwright
5 Highway sign
6 "__ boy!"
7 "The Love for
   Three __": Prokofiev
8 Old World
   songbird
9 Blocks or stalls
   intentionally
10 Gurgle's cousin
11 Prong
14 Arabian gulf
15 Parallels
17 College bldg.
23 Parts
25 Very, in Rouen
26 Confront
27 Silly
28 Watched closely

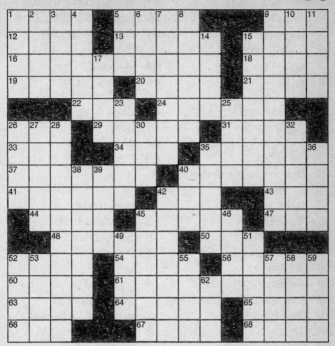

65

30 Soviet chess
   master
32 Harden
35 Tamarack, e.g.
36 On tenterhooks
38 Checked for fiscal
   compliance
39 Cutlet meat
40 "Take __, She's
   Mine," 1961
   Broadway hit
42 Duelists' choice

45 La. patois
46 Air: Comb. form
49 Austen heroine
51 Hot stuff in the
   earth
52 Farm structure
53 Indigo
55 Soon
57 Army food
58 Inclusive abbr.
59 Fast planes
62 Soap ingredient

ACROSS

1 Issue at hand
6 Fighting
11 Pound in
14 T. Jefferson's opponent
15 Motif
16 Ear: Comb. form
17 Categorized
19 Mil. branch
20 Some M.I.T. grads
21 Trouble
22 Webb's police series
24 Cancel a space flight
26 "Rome was not built __"
27 Hired assassin
30 Badger
32 Walking __ (elated)
33 Prefix with physical
34 Wrestling hold
37 Chum
38 Hut: Slang
41 What's the good word, Renée?
42 Printing items
44 City on the Oka
45 ". . . pleasure dome with caves __!"
47 English flower
49 Temporarily
50 Knight's attendant
52 Statue with limitations
54 The why and wherefore

56 Wye chaser
57 Mary Todd's man
60 Fine, at NASA
61 Jingoistic about the U.S.
64 Map abbr.
65 Famed Swiss mathematician
66 Back front
67 Book end?
68 Win by __
69 Frivolous

DOWN

1 Reel thing
2 Tony's cousin
3 Snub-nosed dogs
4 Dudgeon
5 Levers
6 "__ Fair Hands": Davison poem
7 However, for short
8 Actress Tuesday
9 Dreiser's "An __ Tragedy"
10 Household pest
11 Type of tournament
12 Uncertain
13 TV emcee Hall
18 High time
23 British slammer
24 "__ my brother's keeper?"
25 "__ Things in Life Are Free"
27 Pueblo Indian
28 __ instant

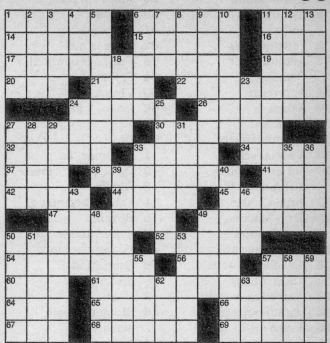

66

29 Mean business
31 Kin of etc.
33 Slight
35 Chanel's nickname
36 Was acquainted with
39 Folksy
40 Score of zero
43 Water vessel
46 To's opposite
48 ". . . I __ mother in Israel": Judges

49 Astaire or Allen
50 Kindle
51 Allotment
53 __ Ike of comics
55 Perry's creator
57 Like some wines
58 Practiced blackmail
59 Counting-out rhyme start
62 Common Market initials
63 Onassis nickname

ACROSS

1 __ and chain
5 Inchoative verb suffix
9 Petty quarrel
13 Antoinette or Osmond
14 Approach
15 Ashen
16 Confused
17 Colombian city
18 A social sci.
19 Act impetuously, N.R.A. style?
22 Public house
23 John Madden exclamation
24 O.S.S. successor
25 Acted impetuously, N.R.A. style?
31 Walked nervously
34 Leguminous plants
35 Wrath
36 Stately steed
37 Plant louse
39 Heavenly spirit, in Lille
40 Rotary device
41 Notion
42 Tony Randall TV role
43 Impetuous, N.R.A. style?
47 Comprehend
48 __ Alamos
49 Health resort
52 Act impetuously, N.R.A. style?
58 Sow one's __ oats
59 V.I.P.'s vehicle
60 Fanon
61 Not aweather
62 "Woe is me!"
63 Used a stopwatch
64 Foreman
65 Vivacious
66 Go to __ (deteriorate)

DOWN

1 __ Rouge, La.
2 Pyromaniac's crime
3 Gladly
4 Foliage beginning
5 Bivouac
6 Authenticate
7 Young elephant
8 Greenland discoverer
9 Coin
10 Shipping-room activity
11 Spiny plant
12 Look after
13 Visitors to infant Jesus
20 Noah's second son
21 Newspaperman Adolph
25 Confederate general Stuart
26 Hebrew unit of dry measure
27 __ gratia (by the grace of God)
28 Minor minor

134

29 Exhort	**45** Nearly
30 __-do-well	**46** Poker prize
31 Treaty	**49** Put to __ (outdo)
32 Moroccan tree	**50** Like some carpets
33 Ladies' underwaists	**51** Mimicked
37 Indiana wit	**52** Mop the deck
38 Through	**53** Hawaiian seaport
39 Some	**54** Tab
41 "__ a Kick Out of	**55** Anger
You"	**56** Poet Khayyam
42 Results	**57** Shallowest of the
44 Crystalline stones	Great Lakes

ACROSS

1 Some coins
6 Pother
10 Verge
14 Kanaga Island language
15 Mandlikova of tennis
16 Floribunda, e.g.
17 Blackmore's Exmoor girl
19 Concern of Niels Bohr
20 Palter
21 Romberg's "The __ Moon"
22 A marble
23 Where Bhutan is
25 Scott's tragic bride
29 Marsh plant
31 Kensington Gardens sights
32 Elect
33 Certain votes
35 Volga feeder
36 Early auto
37 Hemingway's lost lady
41 Baden-Baden, e.g.
43 Soak, as flax
44 Fall behind
45 Equality
46 Some skirts
48 Wandered
52 Tarkington's small-town girl
55 Vedic ritual drink
56 Nureyev, for one
57 Comic Olsen
59 Module for Armstrong
60 A party to
61 Thackeray's adventuress
65 Teen's concern
66 Other
67 Slight color
68 Grant and Marvin
69 Unfledged bird
70 Stage direction

DOWN

1 Diva Maria
2 Plaza denizen
3 Sea nymph
4 Cask
5 Kenton or Laurel
6 Appear
7 The way, in China
8 Hostelry
9 "Norma __"
10 "Erin go __"
11 Revolving
12 U-235 is one
13 Ticket stub, perhaps
18 __ Rio, Tex.
22 Kiang
24 Culture medium
26 Zagreb is its capital
27 Oxen of Tibet
28 Menotti hero
30 Word with evil or naked
34 Narrow groove
37 Nelson Eddy was one

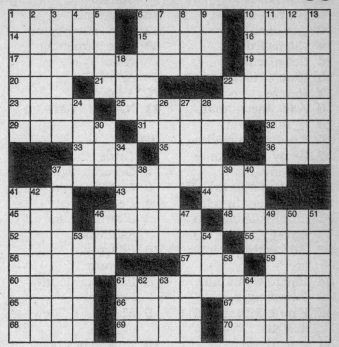

68

38 Wait on
39 Roman household god
40 Psychoanalysts' concerns
41 Having three dimensions
42 Actor Jack from Pa.
46 Debussy's "La __"
47 Stogies, e.g.
49 With wings extended

50 Become manifest
51 Furnace part
53 Walking sticks
54 Cunning
58 Italian princely family
61 Apiary inhabitant
62 English cathedral city
63 Jeff Davis's org.
64 Hebrew liquid measure

ACROSS

1 Foreheads
6 Bureau finisher
10 Qualified
14 Citrus fruit
15 Submarine
16 Kind of table or hall
17 Revere
18 And others: abbr.
19 __ Raton, Fla.
20 Erudite via reading
23 Krazy __ of comics
24 Recent
25 Mottled appearance
27 Ornament in relief
31 Like some modern music
33 Bird with a weird cry
34 Italian commune
36 Plumbing, e.g.
39 Fabric with raised designs
41 Apparition
43 Requested
44 The Charleses' pet
46 Voracious teleosts
47 Swell
49 A semihard yellow cheese
51 Like the Mohawk Trail
53 "It's __ to Tell a Lie"
55 Eureka!
56 Text supporters
62 __ monster
64 Bring up

65 Wild female water buffalo
66 Uniform
67 Pale yellow-green
68 Do a gardening chore
69 Antitoxins
70 A lot
71 Native of Gävle

DOWN

1 Tattle
2 Decorate again
3 Melville novel
4 Be employed
5 Short lines for fishhooks
6 Sharper
7 Asylum
8 Island in County Donegal
9 El Greco's "View of __"
10 Emergency pol. message
11 Set of ex libris
12 Not express
13 Make happy
21 Alleviated
22 Author of "Divina Commedia"
26 Package
27 Site of Napoleon's first exile
28 Humus layers
29 Volume vendor
30 __ a blue moon

138

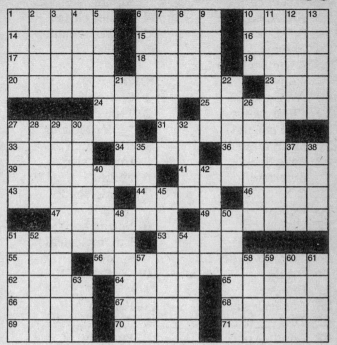

69

32 Touchstone
35 Capital
37 Ready-to-eat food store
38 Formerly, once
40 Extempore
42 Place for a cookout
45 Fleshy plant of the mustard family
48 Future oaks
50 Relatives by marriage
51 Magi

52 Plant related to the onion
54 Petruchio's Katharina
57 Trompe l' __ (visual deception)
58 Sketch
59 Chap, fellow: Sp.
60 Pearl Buck's "The Living __"
61 Withered
63 Table-talk collection

ACROSS

1 Pts. of cars
5 NASA, e.g.
9 S.D.I. targets
14 Radiate
15 Adjective for some gametes
16 Water wheel
17 Prevaricator
18 Part of C.P.U.
20 Marital kin
22 Poke one's __ (interfere)
23 CD
26 Delicate
27 Unspoken
32 Part of VCR
36 "Mondo Cane" hit theme
37 Baptize
38 Nonecclesiastical
41 TV's "__ of Duty"
42 Another part of VCR
43 Rye fungus
45 Word in a closing
46 Beginning of r.p.m.
52 German film about a clay statue: 1920
56 Very bad
57 Characteristic of FM or AM
60 Black, to Calpurnia
61 Chronicle
62 Start of TV

63 "__ we forget . . .": Kipling
64 Comes closer
65 Q.E.D. member
66 Patella

DOWN

1 Souvenir
2 Type of acid
3 "__ for Murder"
4 It's a cinch
5 Unit of elec.
6 Forbid
7 Young comic heroine
8 Spring back
9 Entomological specimen
10 "__ Cosa," 1935 song
11 Fan rib
12 Julep ingredient
13 Pudding thickener
19 Sam has one
21 Thin, crisp cake
24 Places for atts.
25 Bollingen Prize winner: 1957
28 Tatar Strait feeder
29 Algid
30 Dies __
31 Geog. region
32 Quote
33 Cupid

140

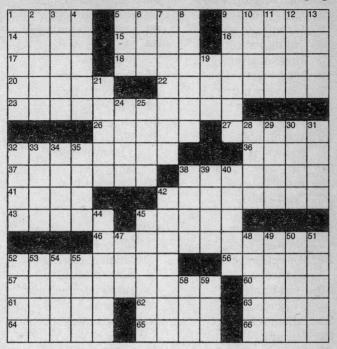

70

34 Self-satisfied
35 Virologist's comb. form
38 Pas __ (solo dance)
39 Beige
40 __ Rica, C.A.
42 More spacious
44 Fishes on the move
45 Actress Mimieux
47 Old scale topper
48 "__ the Line," Cash smash

49 Frequently
50 Kind of shark
51 Blackboard material
52 One of the Feds
53 Sharpen
54 Novelist Ferber
55 Forage legume
58 Biographer Winslow
59 Snood, e.g.

ACROSS

1 Jazz-singing form
5 Johnny on the __
9 Act without words
13 Uninteresting
15 Russian river
16 Seed covering
17 Like very much
18 Cheers for a matador
19 Abominable Snowman
20 They have "darling buds"
22 Draft status
23 Otherwise
24 Popular puzzle birds
26 "Sweet home" for Eastwood
30 First name of 44 Across
31 Samoan seaport
32 Summit
35 One who is wholly holy
39 Diarist Samuel
41 A Gypsy who rose via few clothes
42 __ miss (at random)
43 Proficient
44 Actor in "Same Time, Next Year"
46 Brain, in Barcelona
47 Buck heroine
49 Thought
51 Tinge
53 Danube feeder
55 A spice
56 "In the merry __"
62 Rumanian city
63 French department
64 Metallic waste product
65 Part of a casa
66 Lively dance
67 Uncanny
68 Linger
69 When luters outnumbered computers
70 It's shed in a woodshed

DOWN

1 Make-believe
2 Musical closing
3 Nautical salute
4 Horse-racing track
5 Retards
6 West Indies volcano
7 Lulu
8 Corn part
9 Salad component
10 Personification of peace
11 Chiggers
12 Famed literary pseudonym
14 Scuffle
21 Mexican stew or jar
25 Madcap
26 Matador's apparel
27 Imitated
28 Fully developed

142

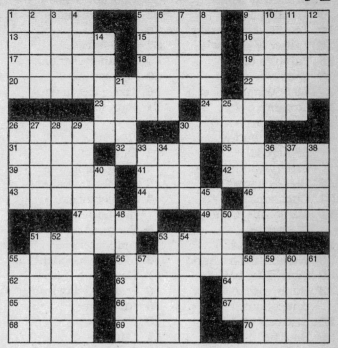

1	2	3	4		5	6	7	8		9	10	11	12
13				14		15					16			
17						18					19			
20					21						22			
			23					24	25				
26	27	28	29				30						
31				32	33	34			35		36	37	38
39			40		41				42				
43				44			45		46				
	47	48				49	50						
51	52				53	54							
55			56	57				58	59	60	61		
62			63				64						
65			66				67						
68			69				70						

29 Springtime celebration, to some
30 Cut
33 Scheme
34 Conger
36 Part of many a column
37 Proboscis
38 Walked upon
40 Capital of Manche
45 Biblical wife
48 Mil. depot

50 Destroy slowly
51 Gemologist's concern
52 Fla. city
53 More secret
54 Monument slab
55 Conglomerate
57 Mountain: Comb. form
58 Irritate
59 Additional
60 Where Brunei is
61 North Sea feeder

ACROSS

1 Broadway bomb
5 Tropical lizard
10 Tennis ace Wilander
14 Father of Hel
15 Fabius's 557
16 Quiz
17 43,560 square feet
18 Low dive
19 Blackthorn
20 With 22 and 58 Across, bakery-window sign
22 See 20 Across
23 Cuckoopint
24 Memorable Chiang __-shek
26 Knucklehead
29 William Tell's canton
30 Typewriter bar
35 Honey-pecan confections
38 Eritrea's capital
39 Boot tie
40 Eve-making material
42 Tall tales
43 Carol starter
45 Relative of a cobbler
47 Xanthippe, e.g.
48 "I __ great eater . . .": Shak.
49 But, to Brutus
50 Genetic inits.
52 Appropriate
54 Own up
58 See 20 Across
63 Expensive
64 Hemingway's "movable feast"
65 Religious image
66 Zilch
67 In reserve
68 Japanese sandal
69 Fall setting
70 Like glass houses
71 Rapt in reverence

DOWN

1 Glitch
2 Lomond, for one
3 Gumbo ingredient
4 Michelangelo masterpiece
5 Suspend a meeting until later
6 More despondent
7 Eager
8 Byelorussian hub
9 River isle
10 Network
11 Car bar
12 Western art colony
13 Captain Hook's henchman
21 Knave of Heart's preference?
22 Englishman's wine-soaked dessert
25 High __ kite
26 Chair-back piece
27 Pedro's plowed land
28 Harness-race horse
31 Nanking nanny
32 Cavils

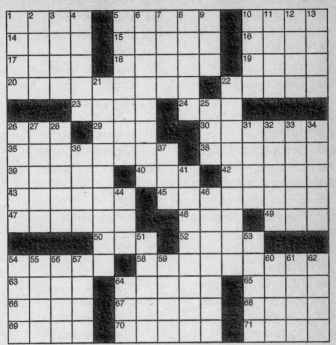

72

33 Kovacs or Ford
34 Brought down the
   house, in Kew
36 "__ we forget":
   Kipling
37 Wee drink
41 Dante's love
44 Deserving bird?
46 Piled up
51 Iowan church
   society
53 Miss Doolittle

54 Carpenter's tool
55 Exploit
56 Grown-up filly
57 Keep a pressing
   engagement
59 "Mourning Becomes
   Electra" man
60 Clumsy boat
61 Drill
62 Writer Bagnold
64 How the weasel
   goes

ACROSS

1 Waft
6 Cicatrix
10 Cobblers
14 Studio stand
15 Irish
16 Killer whale
17 Macaw
18 French number
19 Spree
20 Get a sound sleep
22 Exclusive shop
24 Letters at Calvary
26 Salon specialty
27 They have listings
31 Subway gates
35 French pronoun
36 Gloria __
38 Film: Comb. form
39 Spanish greeting
40 __ a time
41 Bounder
42 Speech problem
44 High point for Moses
45 Ceremony
46 Range of Minn.
48 Exercise-bike adjunct
50 Charlie Brown's expression
52 Easy task
53 More comely
57 Purposeful gait
61 Desolate, once
62 Unprejudiced
64 Vacancy sign
65 Ron Howard TV role
66 Number of feline lives
67 Happening
68 Cervine creature
69 Popular Anglo-Nigerian singer
70 Change colors

DOWN

1 Pal of wash
2 Hopping herbivore
3 "The corn __ high . . ."
4 Fruitful
5 Show off
6 Amex overseer
7 Place for corn
8 Like __ (probably)
9 Formal demands
10 Prudent
11 Basra's locale
12 Color of unbleached linen
13 Eastern beverage
21 They get voted on
23 Trotyl, for short
25 Tabriz native
27 Sphere

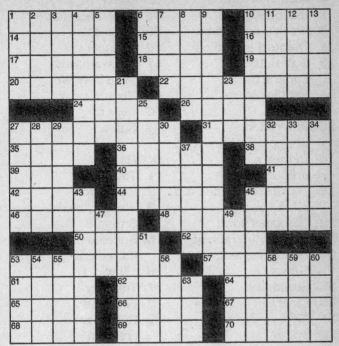

73

28 Ewing matriarch
29 At __ for words
30 Pool member
32 Legitimate
33 Related maternally
34 Hebrew feast
37 Electric catfish
43 Penn, to Teller
45 Chide
47 Leatherwing

49 Make a difference
51 Photo finish
53 Trudge
54 Hitchcock film
55 Mercyhurst College site
56 Tear
58 "__ Three Lives"
59 Refute
60 Small suffix
63 Maiden-named

ACROSS

1 Pakula or Bates
5 Intimidate
8 Week's-end shout
12 Daiquiri ingredient
13 Sub-detection apparatus
15 Role for Marie Wilson
16 Pub orders
17 Shopper's concern
18 Carson's predecessor
19 Tennessee Ernie Ford hit of the 50's
22 Compass point
23 Varnish ingredient
24 Denounce as a failure
26 Summary
29 Emerson products
31 A.F.L.'s partner
32 Spiral
34 Boy Scouts' outings
36 Ampersands
38 Unbroken
40 Break
41 Stitch again
43 Immigrants' island
45 "__ pro nobis"
46 Makes off with
48 Current __
50 It, in Italia
51 __ nutshell
52 __ Lanka
54 Type of typing

61 Trademark
63 Swell
64 Green vegetable
65 Copied
66 Redacts
67 A Karamazov
68 "The Way We __"
69 Rheine's river
70 "Eye of __ . . .": Shak.

DOWN

1 Too bad!
2 Caron role
3 Wall St. board
4 Snuggle
5 Succotash ingredient
6 "Step __!"
7 Tex. city
8 Pinnacle
9 Boy Scout's creation
10 "__ Old Cowhand"
11 Hansom fee
13 Sort
14 Tears
20 "Into __ life . . ."
21 Window part
25 __ oui!
26 Yearns
27 Star of "The Pawnbroker"
28 Plumlike fruits
29 Bonaparte's punishment

30 Roebuck's partner

31 Reo or Stutz

33 Sick

35 Hot springs

37 Espies

39 Intuits

42 Launder

44 Transmit

47 "To a __," Burns poem

49 Table-linen piece

52 Side dish

53 Funambulist's footing

55 Bare

56 Crop

57 Reps.

58 Roof part

59 Tabby's defense

60 Superman's surname

62 Keats's creation

ACROSS

1 Spinning material
6 Speedily
11 Sea cow
13 Rock-clinging mollusk
15 Garlands for the head
16 U.S. W.W. II rifles
17 Rather
18 Foil or pan preceder
20 G.I. resting place
21 Member of a Panay people
22 One-seeded fruits
26 Sooner than
27 Cambridge inst.
28 British show place
29 Neighbor of Leb.
30 Soho O
32 Capitol body
34 Fold matron
35 Fixed-term bank accts.
36 Gemology measures
39 Purloins
42 Touching game
43 Poisonous snake
45 Raises
47 Egg: Comb. form
48 Needlewomen's needs
49 Small Tibetan antelope
50 Winebibber
51 Devour
52 Visceral
53 Attends uninvited
57 Spring
61 Gains
62 Impaired
63 Used 48 Across
64 Stormed

DOWN

1 Zealot
2 Fatuity
3 Naughty
4 Hot time for Pierre
5 Ad __ (to the point)
6 Saudi garment
7 Eagle plus two
8 Neighbor of Ga.
9 Vanity
10 Approve of publicly
11 Palindromic lady
12 Mordecai's cousin
13 Insurance sellers
14 Homophone for 12 Down
19 New Yorker cartoonist
22 Crosswise
23 Leopard's kin

75

24 Put up
25 Mailers
31 __ capita
33 Mad __ hatter
36 Romps about
37 Shake up
38 Symptom of
overwork
39 Did a roofing job
40 Traveler's need
41 Declaimed

42 Puccini work:
1900
44 Souchong, for one
46 Too full
54 Crosscut
55 Get a move on
56 Split or tight Jet
58 Spoil
59 "I __ Camera"
60 Emulate
Xanthippe

ACROSS

1 It's a laugh
5 __-a-brac
9 Scads
13 Twenty: Comb. form
15 "Splitsville"
16 Secrete
17 Rigor
19 Leave out
20 In place of
21 Diner sign
22 Hosp. group
23 Yak
25 Evicts
29 Philosopher Jean-Paul
32 "Lord, __ I?": Matt. 26:22
33 Marmosets of S. America
35 Concerning drugs
39 One after another
40 Actress Naldi
41 Wandered
42 Jack Webb program of yore
45 Card game
46 Author Fleming
47 Skillful
50 Marry
54 Affirm confidently
55 Very nervous
58 Salami haven
59 Prod
60 Blue planet

61 A Guthrie
62 Chow
63 A pope who became a saint

DOWN

1 Word on a towel
2 Play starter
3 Unicorn feature
4 Hoffman play: 1985
5 Chicken part
6 Tear
7 Corp. abbreviation
8 Like Marvell's mistress
9 Small sum
10 Bean or city
11 Redact
12 Volstead's opponents
14 Musical beginning
18 Knee, to a zoologist
23 United: Comb. form
24 Berlin's "He's __ Picker"
25 Card spots
26 Wedding aide
27 Crown of a sort
28 A combo
29 Maglie or Mineo
30 Castor-bean product
31 Related to Mom

76

33 Piper's son
34 Wooden strip
36 Epiphany threesome
37 Egyptian sun disk
38 Spanish hero, with "El"
42 Plates
43 Séance sounds
44 Swinburne's "___ on Charlotte Bronte"

47 Art style
48 Eternally
49 Flopped
50 Roe
51 Russian river
52 Positive
53 Within: Comb. form
55 Top sound
56 Fury
57 F-J connection

ACROSS

1 Information
5 "Shoo!"
9 Degrade
14 Aid a criminal
15 "The Sun __ Rises"
16 Boner
17 Bedstead part
18 Crawford film from a Maugham work
19 Carpenter's need
20 TV part for Stacy Keach
22 Bracken or Fisher
23 Female red deer
24 Chew the fat
25 Recorded, in a way
28 Supposed
33 Actress Lupino
34 Pilfered
37 Function
38 Country-club sport
40 Close, to Cowper
41 Christmas
42 Columnist Bombeck
43 Weighing machines
45 Morose
46 Arose as a consequence
48 Journalists
50 Prevaricate
51 Peter, Paul and Mary, e.g.
53 Bandleader Jones
56 "Cannery Row" author

61 Lengthwise
62 Canvas covering at Shea Stad.
63 Presage
64 In India, a reigning queen
65 Otherwise
66 Fatigue
67 Knots in wood
68 Part of a hammer's head
69 Goulash, e.g.

DOWN

1 Dollop
2 Competent
3 Bad News Bears, e.g.
4 Clothes
5 Bilko's rank, for short
6 Talons
7 Largest continent
8 Actor Danza
9 Defender of Troy
10 Noted sci-fi author
11 Dry
12 Performances by one person
13 Irish Gaelic
21 Affirmative motions
24 Type
25 "Save the __," Lemmon film
26 Worship

154

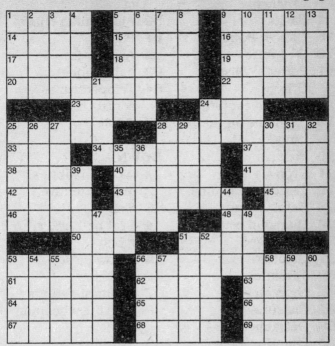

77

27 "The Wild __," book
   by 39 Down
28 Beg
29 Genuine
30 Mickey or Minnie
31 Greece, to Greeks
32 Actions
35 Flavor
36 Formerly
39 Creator of the
   Snopes family
44 Rotate

47 Vassals
49 Automatons
51 Succinct
52 Mature
53 Scotsman's shirt
54 Scheme
55 Variety of grape
56 Gait
57 Malamud product
58 Give off
59 Part of a bird's beak
60 Was aware of

ACROSS

1 Cracker
8 Sacks
15 Dancer Powell
16 Obdurate
17 Porter's "Miss Otis __"
18 Brahms cantata
19 It's home on the range
20 Plexus
21 Crop
22 Cartoonist Hulme
23 Bambi's aunt
25 Diamond cover
26 Witnessed
27 Galatea's love
30 Faulkner character
31 Caesura
33 Declaimed
35 Like Burnett's jungle
37 Allot
41 Plane of W.W. I
45 Two taker
46 Sonoran Indian
47 Got a hole-in-one
49 Kiss-and-__
50 Bus. org. of W.W. II
52 Oar: Comb. form
53 Prefix for center
54 Profligate
57 Oscar winner of 1970
59 Algonquian chiefs
61 Pig out
62 Apprentice
63 Tab grabber
64 Temperature-control devices
65 Futile

DOWN

1 Worsted fabrics
2 More attentive
3 Heir
4 Crabbe-Barker roles
5 Arrow poison
6 __ Dame
7 Hesitant sounds
8 Like the whooping crane
9 Entrance
10 Weathercock
11 Org. with a journal
12 Dashing
13 Sanction
14 Quashed
20 Risen Star is one
24 British baby's diaper
25 Chinese pagoda
28 Noted rug weavers

156

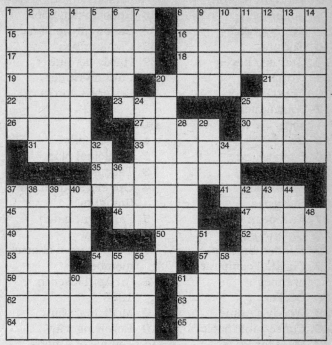

78

29 Impresario Hurok
32 Pitch
34 Part of E.R.A.
36 Louis and Lawrence
37 Bears witness
38 Forearm
39 Creole State bird
40 Olive or Castor
42 Biased
43 Synthetic fabric

44 Busts
48 RR cars
51 Boxes
54 It rhymes with keno
55 Tenth of an ephah
56 Applications
58 Fit to __
60 Towel word
61 R-V connection

ACROSS

1 Petulant person
5 Sonoran sandwiches
10 Endure
14 Utah ski haven
15 Worship
16 Countertenor
17 Tournament of sorts
19 Brio
20 Slow-witted
21 Scrap heap
23 .9144 meter
26 Straggles
27 European viper
30 Unfettered
32 Sudden breezes
36 Cocktail component, at times
38 Declare
39 Woody's Annie
40 Coffee-table book
42 Piece for Price
43 Occurs afterward
45 "Naked Came a __": 1969
47 Charger
48 Joe Friday's grist
49 Winter time in N.Y.C.
50 Indonesian island
52 Security device
54 Schussboomer's turn
58 Set straight
62 Region
63 Temperamental person
66 Russian neighbor
67 Shoot-em-up film
68 Cloak or boa
69 Hardy heroine
70 Captain Butler
71 Performs stitchery

DOWN

1 City division
2 Medicinal plant
3 Take aback
4 Ophelia's flower "for thoughts"
5 Pavement patch
6 Foofaraw
7 Cooperstown charter member
8 An April loser in 1988
9 Medicinal plant
10 Revolving tray
11 Temple of Athena __
12 Pentacle
13 Passed the word
18 Passes the pasteboards
22 __ Benedict
24 Chimney neighbors
25 Extinct bird
27 Aspirin targets
28 Viewpoint
29 Beat
31 Mexican's hot sauce
33 Suit material
34 Essays

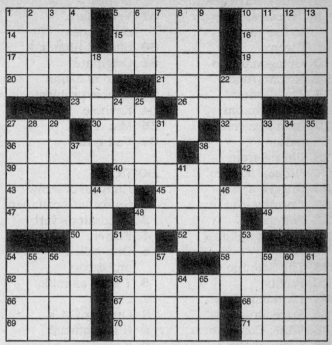

79

35 Outset
37 Informal attire
38 Major body vessel
41 Scratcher's target
44 Dutch cheese
46 Hafez al-__, Syrian President
48 Actress Fawcett
51 Inhalant
53 Farm implements

54 Only President to sit on the Supreme Court
55 N.Y. county
56 Camera-bag item
57 Carnivorous bird
59 Concerning
60 Nobble ceaselessly
61 Dagwood's delights
64 Strawberry or Darling, once
65 __ Deco

ACROSS

1 Unattractive feature
5 "These studies are __ to the young . . .": Cicero
10 Octagonal sign
14 Roman road
15 Timid one
16 Meerschaum
17 Item in a certain parlor
18 Phrase from "Robert's Rules"
20 Suggests
22 Dorothy, to Em
23 Palters
24 Post for a ship's line
26 The Scourge of God
29 Profits
33 Danke, in Dijon
34 Price for poker
35 Wine: Comb. form
36 __ nutshell
37 With 28 Down, business association
40 Hilo floral arrangement
41 Gently bob
42 One
43 Falters
45 Chests of drawers
47 Give
48 Raison d'__
49 Niblick, e.g.
50 Use a rapier

53 Away from the mouth
57 Veto's fate, sometimes
60 Sitarist Shankar
61 Originate
62 Kind of drum
63 Faucet problem
64 Keyhole
65 Markets
66 Vail gear

DOWN

1 Handful of straw
2 Suffix with comment
3 Decorator's verb
4 Barter
5 One-celled protozoan
6 Turns, as milk
7 Places
8 Org. for G.I.'s
9 N.F.L. official
10 Elf
11 This might be red
12 Kuwait, Qatar, etc.
13 Le __ Noël
19 Up for debate, as a bill
21 Legislative tactic
24 Sergeant Pepper's group
25 Analogy-test words
26 "A heart unfortified, __ impatient": Shak.
27 Purport
28 See 37 Across

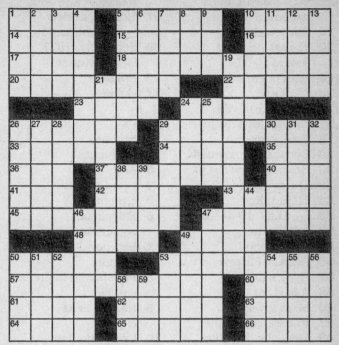

80

29 Transports of
    sorts
30 Ala. city
31 Awkward
32 Cacophony
38 Humdinger
39 River at Leeds
44 Interior parts of
    engines
46 Furtive
47 Stingless, feckless
    bees

49 "Le Roi d'Yvetot"
    composer
50 Moat
51 Pernicious
52 Infamous fiddler
53 Jewish month
54 Prank
55 Cato's 57
56 Kennel sounds
58 Distinctive
    doctrine
59 Genetic letters

ACROSS

1 U.S. Coast Guard woman
5 Pile neatly
10 Throat-clearing sound
14 Roof edge
15 __ d'hote
16 Opposite of yep
17 British Navy woman
18 Foreigner
19 Speaker of baseball
20 Scarlet weaverbird
23 Ott or Tormé
24 Liquid meas.
25 "__ Hill," 1940 song
30 Auriculate
35 Time period
36 Actress Farrow
37 Eye membrane
38 Assistant
40 Main artery
42 Italian wine center
43 Mentally defective person
45 Son of Gad: Gen. 40:16
46 Moray, e.g.
47 A king of Judea
48 Thanksgiving Day sauce source
51 Ration book agcy.
53 Spanish title
54 Twain novel
63 SW Asian country
64 Proportion
65 Money exchange fee
66 Having all one's marbles
67 Holding device
68 __ and robbers
69 Seattle __, 1977 Derby winner
70 Pulls
71 Gaelic

DOWN

1 Stitches
2 Segment
3 Assert
4 Change a title
5 Groom, e.g.
6 Falsehood, sometimes
7 Red powder used in India
8 Priests and bishops, e.g.
9 Nairobi is its capital
10 Oppositionist
11 Cornucopia
12 Long heroic poem
13 Engage, as gears
21 Spider network
22 Escape
25 Sandy shore
26 River in France
27 Below
28 Ebro is one
29 More unusual
31 Mindanao native
32 Part of a stairway
33 Be admitted

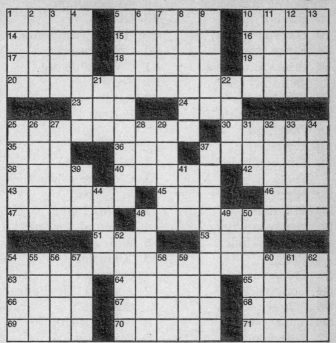

81

34 Bettor's __ double
37 Fallers on
   Bacharach's head
39 Ike's command
41 __-la-la
44 False god
48 Occult doctrine
49 Lad
50 Write on the front
   of a bill
52 Sit
54 Sibilant sound

55 Russian mountain
   range
56 Walking aid
57 "What Maisie __":
   H. James
58 Common Latin abbr.
59 Hoarfrost
60 Sikorsky or
   Stravinsky
61 Bites
62 Kind of cone or
   dive

ACROSS

1 Boone and Sajak
5 Kind of dunk
9 Damage a bolt
14 Exam type
15 Prince Charles's game
16 Fuming
17 Pater, in Paris
18 Overhaul
19 Unvoiced
20 Finney film role: 1982
23 "Cheers" choice
24 Suitable
25 Gypsy language
29 "Desire Under the __"
31 Preserve
34 Construct
35 "Three men in __"
36 "And __ bed"
37 Yule figure
40 Raison d'__
41 Berserk
42 Postpone action on
43 Music's __ Speedwagon
44 Bills featuring G.W.
45 Comic Lloyd
46 Rainbow
47 Family member
48 Stacy Keach TV role
55 Chili spice

56 Actress Winningham
57 On
59 "Love __ the Ruins"
60 Cold desserts
61 Civil-rights org.
62 Scow
63 Assay
64 Portent

DOWN

1 Mom's mate
2 Cézanne's "Boy in __ Vest"
3 O'Hara home
4 Rosebud, for one
5 With agility
6 "Camelot" composer
7 Actor in "The Four Seasons"
8 Secure a ship
9 Exercises
10 Pamphlet
11 Auto lift
12 Medical suffix
13 Darling
21 Italian poet
22 Disney classic
25 Send (to)
26 Emulate Demosthenes
27 Subway in Milano
28 Long
29 Mores
30 Wait in hiding

164

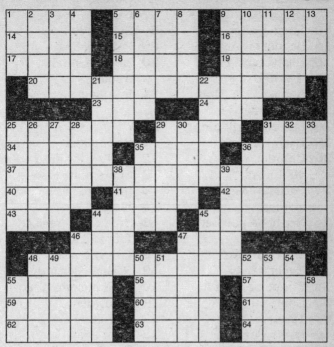

82

31 Jazz group
32 In any way
33 Did some prying
35 High point
36 Leading role
38 Ponderosa, e.g.
39 Squeaky-voiced Arnold
44 A suburb of Newark
45 Genuine
46 Rich Little's forte

47 Horses' male parents
48 Wild cat
49 Love, in Juárez
50 Give off
51 Tear-gas relative
52 Tex. city
53 Smidgen
54 Days of __
55 Truck area
58 Enclosure

ACROSS

1 Theatrical starter
5 Brackets on masts
10 Show leader
14 School event
15 Destructive craft
16 "I would a __ unfold . . .": Shak.
17 Coarse file
18 List of candidates
19 Leafy shaders
20 Creation of 40 Across
23 Porter's "Night and __"
24 Neither's partner
25 Poplar
28 Mild untruth
31 Egypt's river
34 Coupe or sedan
35 Comes up
38 Title
40 Lewis Carroll
43 Josip Broz
44 Addison partner
45 W.W. II theater
46 String follower
48 Opposite of NNE
49 Nostrils
51 Theologian's deg.
53 Johnny __
54 Creation of 40 Across
62 Pro __
63 Military fieldwork
64 Certain poems
66 Ostentatiously esthetic
67 Choose
68 Some bills
69 Pandowdies
70 English sandy tracts
71 Indulge to excess

DOWN

1 Spring mo.
2 Ending for auto
3 Sheer nonsense
4 Interfere with
5 Shaggy
6 Suffix with resist
7 Tropical snakes
8 Tub rub
9 Rathskeller mug
10 Kind of committee
11 A powder
12 __ mater
13 Take five
21 Erie is one
22 White House nickname
25 Bank abbr.
26 Title of respect in Delhi
27 Chatter
28 Fighting tools
29 Emerald and others
30 Moisten, in a way
32 Kind of beam
33 Express effusively

83

36 Legal thing
37 Money in Peru
39 Slaughter of baseball fame
41 Streets, etc.
42 Star in Cygnus
47 A degree
50 Seminary heads
52 Engaged
53 Carries on
54 Links hazard

55 Mata __
56 Diminutive ending
57 Far: Comb. form
58 Statesman or garden
59 Horse or human chaser
60 Thought
61 Big top
65 Wind dir.

ACROSS

1 Circle segments
5 Watch-pocket ribbons
9 Young 'un
12 Strike vigorously
13 G.I. vehicle
14 "__, vidi, vici"
15 Nursery steed
17 Ferber
18 Compass point
19 Apply graffiti
20 Tabloid's grist
22 Withdraws, in a way
25 Actor Donahue
26 Dowel
27 Constitution component
31 Half of a 60's folk quartet
34 Musical for Aquarians
35 Imprecise time unit
36 Rainbow goddess
37 Church notices on matrimony
38 Milk or hand follower
39 Marathon segment
40 Like the Gobi
41 Merits
42 Stragglers
45 Black cuckoo
46 Siberian tent
47 Flag's position, at times

52 Grievance resolver
55 "Tippecanoe and Tyler __"
56 Actress Arthur
57 A sea
58 Bubble-bath denizen
61 Writer Grey
62 Lamb
63 Social grouping
64 Lodge man
65 Super Bowl XX M.V.P.
66 Flock members

DOWN

1 How Lindy flew
2 Vestments
3 Tinker, Evers or Chance
4 Causes frustration
5 Norwegian sea arm
6 Poetic adverb or preposition
7 Mrs. Truman
8 Shades
9 Childhood keepsake
10 Pavlova
11 Rheostat's control
12 "Mask" star
14 Harsh criticism
16 Droop
21 Altar in the sky
23 Audit makers
24 __ Main
28 Citrus peel

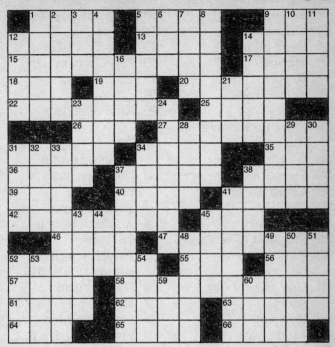

29	Prime beef cut	44	Actor Carney
30	Some pass receivers	45	Medicinal plant
31	Unpleasant person	48	Facing the pitcher
32	__ rug	49	Treat with disdain
33	Fortune starter?	50	Religious groups
34	Rocklike	51	Gambling profit
37	Operated at a bazaar	52	Cutting tool
38	Deform in battle	53	__ estate
41	Carry out	54	Sit on the throne
43	Pathfinder	59	Coal holder
		60	Grackle

ACROSS

1 Appease
5 Fiascoes
10 Lincoln's coin
14 Drug plant
15 Mature
16 Repute
17 Actor Bruce
18 Kind of car
19 Place for broken matches
20 Steering device
22 Put on a happy face
24 Colorless liquid
25 Plot
27 O.K.: Var.
29 Picasso or Casals
33 Kind of tide or water
35 Unit of heat, for short
36 Dormant
37 Kind of can
38 AMPAS award
40 Inebriated
41 Lustrous gems
44 Midwest inst.
45 Mormons: abbr.
46 Phoebe
47 Absolute
50 Nosegays
52 Violet, e.g.
55 Like some Irish eyes
58 Governing body
59 Israeli dance
60 Ralph Kramden's mate
63 Slap aftermath
64 "Once __ . . ."
65 Role for 11 Down
66 Legendary villain
67 Circus item
68 __ clear of
69 Kind of glass

DOWN

1 Training group
2 Northern islands native
3 William Joyce
4 Austrian botanist: 1822-84
5 British novelist-editor: 1850-1912
6 Harem room
7 Kind of pie
8 Plant disorder
9 Five-and-ten, e.g.
10 Of an eye part
11 Actress Barbara
12 Not at all
13 Stepped on
21 Be human
23 Some kids
25 N.C.O.s
26 Sound of amusement
28 Nigerian tribe
30 Hearty guffaw
31 Sorrow, to Schumann

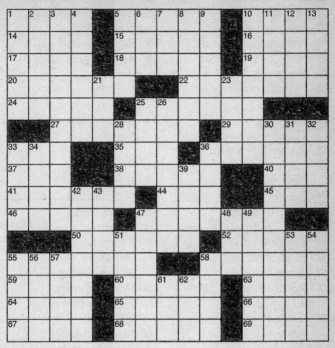

85

32 Chooses
33 Finland native
34 "__ how narrow . . .":
   Rilke
36 __ for one's money
39 Chemical endings
42 Sow anew
43 Pope: 440-61
47 Small porker
48 Expert
49 Sonata
   movements

51 Obstacles
53 Alamogordo's
   county
54 Find another
   tenant
55 Close
56 Sulk
57 Kind of horse
58 Diviner
61 Paul or Joseph
   follower
62 Fr. company

ACROSS

1 Beer ingredient
5 Blunder
10 Fastener
14 Hebrew instrument
15 Web-footed female
16 Voice range
17 Tall, skinny person
19 Gist
20 Sorrow
21 Those who osculate
23 Numerical suffix
24 "Olympia" painter
25 Seventh Greek letter
28 Bristle
30 British trolley
33 Predicate part
35 Sly look
37 Kind of wave
39 Sealed vial
41 Era in Europe: 1000 B.C.-A.D. 100
43 Produce numerous issue
44 Spouse
46 Happy look
47 Greek peak
48 NaCl
50 External: Comb. form
51 Kilmer classic
54 Indonesian island group
56 Shoe cleaner
59 Two long syllables in poetry
63 Hindu queen
64 Very small bankroll
66 ". . . as __ gathereth her chickens . . .": Matt. 23:37
67 Weird
68 Sondheim's "__ the Woods"
69 Village
70 Yukon vehicles
71 Turns right, as a horse

DOWN

1 Bulk
2 Nick and Nora's dog
3 Nobleman
4 Threefold
5 Yellowish-white
6 Plunders
7 Sturgeon egg
8 Honshu seaport
9 Enzyme formed in kidneys
10 Knee tendon
11 Toward shelter, at sea
12 Asterisk
13 Cooking utensils
18 Clears, as profit
22 Argument
24 __ West, of old films
25 Marton and Tanguay
26 Rate of speed
27 Harps, in Havana
29 Abound
31 Antarctic cape

172

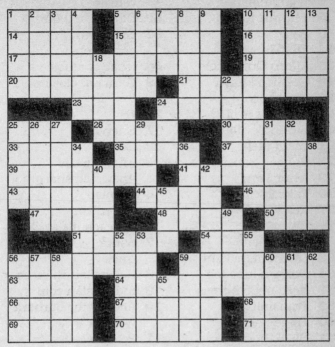

86

32 __ Johnson of N.B.A. fame
34 Archer's need
36 __ Gam, actress from Pa.
38 Fasting period
40 Deprive of weapons
42 Backslides
45 Silly person
49 Horse's gait
52 Facilitates
53 Waters or Barrymore

55 Strip of equipment
56 Dull
57 Chief Hawaiian island
58 Something unique
59 One of the Turkomans
60 Wine and __
61 Being, in Madrid
62 Selves
65 Mining find

ACROSS

1 Wound mark
5 Tell-tale tellers
10 Sour
14 First-rate
15 Aileen Quinn role
16 Fast-food fizzer
17 Insurance, e.g.
19 Was aware of
20 Sir, in Sevilla
21 Giant Mel
22 Range roamer
23 Actor Torn
25 Takeoff
27 Reading desk
31 Church instrument
33 Lotion ingredient
34 Doing a lube job
37 Need of 68 Across
39 Transmit
40 Treads heavily
41 Blackthorn
42 Explosive
43 Weak
44 Quaker William
45 "Tempest" sprite
47 Boxed
49 Treated badly
52 Sailor
53 Receded
55 Actress Scala
57 Sag
61 Zoo sound
62 Owner
64 Skirt style
65 Judith Anderson vehicle
66 Barrett or Jaffe
67 Gershwin portrayer
68 Isaac of music
69 Garment closing

DOWN

1 Enervates
2 Center
3 After a while
4 Answered sharply
5 Varnish ingredient
6 "__ each life . . ."
7 Santa __, Calif. track
8 Noisy disturbances
9 Indonesian coin
10 Activity for Barbara Walters
11 Peacekeepers
12 Thought: Comb. form
13 Early morning
18 Pa. port of entry
22 TV's Gertrude
24 Urges onward
26 Permission
27 At the end of the line
28 Verdugo of "Marcus Welby, M.D."
29 Illegally transported goods

174

87

30 Christie's "Death on the __"
32 Nary a soul
35 Evert maneuver
36 Relaxing
38 Travel
41 Bout rehearsers
43 Ongoing hostility
46 European peninsula
48 Moslem judge
50 Plumed heron
51 Electron tube
53 Writer Bombeck
54 Bring to a bubble
56 Mimic
58 Midwestern tribesman
59 Chaplin's widow
60 Baby buggy
62 A.M. followers
63 Operated

ACROSS

1 Sacred bull of Egypt
5 Up in __ (indignant)
9 French or Melba follower
14 Traditional knowledge
15 Tempt
16 At the right moment
17 Summit
18 Actress Samms
19 City on the St. Lawrence
20 Fabricates
22 Aviary inhabitants
24 Sappho creation
25 Harry James hit record
28 D.C. gun lobby
29 Bobbins
32 Boxing great
35 __ Park, Colo.
39 Sever
40 Reeve-Seymour film, 1980
44 Roman Catholic leader
45 Capital of Bangladesh, old style
46 Adage
47 City in ancient Laconia
50 Terminus
52 Dexter Gordon film: 1986

59 Wager
61 More scarce
62 Vicious, coarse person
63 U.F.O. crew member
65 Expression of worry
67 Aladdin's find
68 List of candidates
69 "__ Lisa"
70 Wallet items
71 Type of bar
72 Indigo
73 City on Lake Michigan

DOWN

1 Cottonwood
2 Visit unexpectedly
3 Goddess of peace
4 Church official
5 Honest one
6 Stallone role
7 Ape
8 Desolate
9 Even chance
10 Yoko __
11 Parthenon's site
12 Brought to court
13 Far: Comb. form
21 Fastening device
23 Radio personalities
26 Switch
27 Greatest
30 Capital of Peru
31 Mulligan, e.g.
32 Vipers

176

88

33 Chicago business
   district
34 Fair
36 Knight or
   Danson
37 Period of note
38 N.Y.S.E. watchdog
41 Architect Saarinen
42 Frozen
43 Child's nurse
48 Diverted
49 Santa __, Calif.

51 Conversation
53 Play
54 Cantaloupe
55 Teheran resident
56 W African
   country
57 Four-bagger
58 Stowe grower
59 Orchestra member
60 First lady of scat
64 Greek letter
66 Mineo or Maglie

ACROSS

1 Emulate beavers
5 Fragment
10 Gush forth
14 Shakespearean villain
15 Self-assurance
16 Jacob's third son
17 Old Glory
20 Lift
21 Animal doc.
22 Spacious
23 More orderly
25 Independent
26 Motor coach
28 Frigid
29 Lose force
30 Buttons or Skelton
33 Slenderized
36 Bridge expert Sharif
37 St. __ (Leeward island)
38 Socko!
39 Tee shot
40 Kind of chamber
41 Linguistic forms
43 "Norma __"
44 Type of bread
45 A.F.T. rival
46 Six-pointers
47 Feds
49 Stone foundation
51 "__ Grows in Brooklyn"
53 Spanish aunt
54 Mutton and veal
57 Mortimer Snerd's friend
60 Spiral
61 Fear
62 Bit of news
63 Melody
64 Move sideways
65 Watches

DOWN

1 Lillian of acting fame
2 Alliance letters
3 Displeasing
4 From bad to __
5 Bad Ems, e.g.
6 Fit to be transported
7 Added clause
8 Vice prin., e.g.
9 Favorite
10 Thin mud
11 "Peanuts" character
12 Daredevil Knievel
13 Sagacious
18 Blots
19 Almost unique
24 Fort Worth inst.
25 Topmast support
26 Pieman
27 City in the Empire State
29 Fiendish
31 Like chalet roofs
32 Trim

89

34 Ike's W.W. II command
35 Soviet chess expert
36 Mountain: Comb. form
39 Cosmic order, in Buddhism
41 Author Rand
42 Vigor
44 Stagger
48 Actress Oberon

49 Coated with hoarfrost
50 Eagle's nest
51 Nos. person
52 One grand, for short
53 Actress Garr
55 "Of __ I Sing"
56 Sylvia __, British leading lady
58 Psyche parts
59 Alphabetic trio

ACROSS

1. "Thy word is __ unto my feet"
6. Pretty girl: Slang
10. Baal, for one
14. Farr who played Klinger
15. Sweeten the pot
16. San __, Riviera resort
17. Herbert's "__ in the Dark"
18. Clock part
19. Last word at church
20. Warning to sailors
23. Orb
24. School org.
25. Sal and Sunday
28. Swabs
31. Was solicitous
36. Altar constellation
37. Notable period
38. Poet Dickinson
39. Time of day to Browning
44. Shaker's partner
45. Tango number
46. Emerger from Adam's rib
47. Precious violin
48. Earth inheritors
49. Mine finds
50. Health club
52. Jabber
54. Berlin's waking sentiments
63. Always
64. Trick
65. Silly
66. Scarce
67. Gaelic
68. Pravda founder
69. "Scots wha hae wi' Wallace __": Burns
70. Appear
71. Limits

DOWN

1. Not fully closed
2. Veronica of films
3. Among
4. Is lonesome for
5. Annoying
6. Art cult
7. "What's __ for me?"
8. Collectors' items
9. Spartan slave
10. Iraqi neighbor
11. Half: Prefix
12. Sign
13. Yearn
21. Red Sea country
22. Big A events
25. Greek letter
26. "__ With a View": Forster
27. Imago, when young

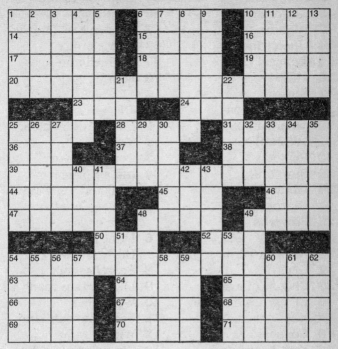

90

29 Assn.
30 Adhesive
32 Soul, in Savoie
33 Columbia or Missouri
34 Pupil, to Pierre
35 Units of force
40 Left, after taxes
41 Hibernians
42 Reverent respect
43 Edo, today
48 Ripe

49 Pried a crate
51 Peels
53 Lithe
54 Basil or tarragon
55 Avocado's shape
56 "If I __ a Rich Man"
57 Angered
58 To exist, to Cato
59 Abound
60 Zest
61 Unicorn fish
62 Writes

ACROSS

1 Norse deity
5 Networks
9 High up
14 Unconvincing
15 Tropical plant
16 Miffed
17 Stress
19 Sport groups
20 American painter: 1887-1986
22 Regret
23 Sun. talk
24 Morse-code character
26 Proverbs
30 Fate
35 River in Turkey
37 Decays
39 Excuse of a sort
40 Bluegrass honorary title
43 Console
44 Flat, broad and thick piece
45 Saucy
46 Staggered
48 Patron saint of Sweden
50 Wall and Broad: abbr.
51 Masonry pin
53 Type of grass
55 Stately fowl?
63 Ruth's mother-in-law
64 Calcutta dungeon
65 Colo. ski resort
66 Windbag
67 __ even keel (steady)
68 Single entity
69 Weddell and Ross
70 Penny

DOWN

1 Cassini of fashion
2 Matron
3 Consequence
4 Indian prime minister: 1947-64
5 "Able __ ere I saw Elba"
6 Lamb's pen name
7 Burly fellow
8 Searches for
9 Like certain roads
10 Willingly
11 Scandinavian king
12 Wife, legally
13 Six-pointers: abbr.
18 Long time
21 Comic book screech
24 Capital of Senegal
25 Goddess of peace
27 Part of a circle
28 Chinese cooking pans
29 Fashion
31 Watery snow
32 Thick soup
33 Chicago-based film critic

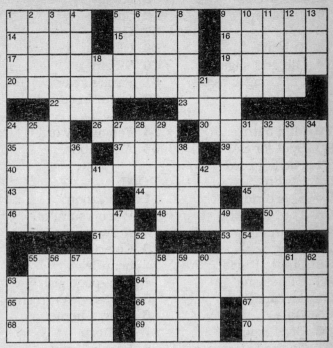

91

34 Slopes
36 Type of aircraft, for short
38 Cicatrix
41 Continuous
42 Sash
47 Buck's mate
49 Hit on the head
52 "Her Nibs" of songdom
54 Type of committee

55 Reckless
56 Pueblo dweller
57 Augur
58 Blackthorn
59 Zhivago's love
60 Experts
61 Verve
62 Fender mishap
63 __ King Cole

ACROSS

1 Betrayed
5 Luminary
9 In re
13 Tub plant
14 Dill and sage
16 Folk singer Ives
17 Meek one
18 Of the eye
19 Mild oath
20 Spot for SAC
21 Playing card
22 Blazing
24 Sharp ridge
26 Thorn
27 Saunter
29 Zone
30 Singer Davis
33 Of hearing
34 An Amerind
35 Gala
36 Brief amour
37 To the left, at sea
39 Until
40 Truncates
41 Small number
42 Jesse James, e.g.
44 Theater sign
45 Bridge
46 Behind a ship
47 Kind of jury
49 Trapshooting
50 Like some autumn
   leaves

52 Biblical book
53 Hwy.
56 Jai __
57 Go in
59 Close
60 Villein
61 Paris's river
62 Autumn colors
63 Nosegay
64 Fencing sword
65 Aide: abbr.

DOWN

1 Casa room
2 Patron saint of
   Norway
3 Colorful fall
   beauties
4 Soc.-page girl
5 Certain evergreens
6 Crow's home
7 Tinhorn
8 Baseball stat.
9 A source of soft
   wood
10 Fall beauties
11 London trolley
12 Ye __ Tea Shoppe
15 Bright-hued fall
   beauty
21 Narrate
23 Healthy
25 Agitates
26 Bar order

92

27 Embarks
28 An English royal house
29 Autumnal color
31 Place of worship
32 Jester
35 Mesa
38 Fuel from bogs
43 Employs
45 Sault __ Marie
48 Enlighten

49 Episode
50 Catch one's breath
51 Spread
52 Alert
54 Boys
55 Formerly, formerly
58 Bess Truman, __ Wallace
59 Blue Eagle org.

ACROSS

1 Transport of a sort
5 One for the plus column
10 Coin catcher
14 Yesterday, to René
15 Get to
16 Singer Seeger
17 Creme Fraiche's jockey: Belmont, 1985
19 Pro __
20 Used-car deal
21 __ Paulo, Brazil
22 Consumer
23 Calabria currency
25 Gothic-window lacework
27 Astronaut's approval
30 Vipers
32 Prior, to Prior
33 Shows appreciation
35 Fortunetelling medium
40 Angelic topper
41 Graceland name
42 "QB VII" penner
43 Streisand hit
45 Swiftly
46 A.F.L.-__
47 Bruce of films
49 By means of
50 Spontaneous action
54 Neural network

56 Chicago business area
57 __ de France
59 Deceived
63 Caron role
64 Jackson nickname
66 __ Islands, off Ireland
67 Dressed to the __
68 Mystery writer Lesley __
69 Weight deduction
70 Browns
71 Garden beauty

DOWN

1 "Moonstruck" star
2 Gal Friday
3 Warm shades
4 Court event
5 Weapon suppliers
6 Baltic, e.g.
7 Enervates
8 Notoriety
9 Formulas
10 Grooms oneself
11 Rent
12 Aquatic mammal
13 Sad-eyed
18 Inventor Howe
24 Rome, for one
26 "Exodus" hero
27 Flu symptom
28 Norwegian monarch
29 Leafy green

186

93

31 Rescued
34 Bristly rodent
36 Ocean greyhound
37 Ensnare
38 Shanghai staple
39 North Sea feeder
41 Deteriorations
44 Hodges or
McDougald
45 Caper
48 Negligent

50 __ ease (nervous)
51 Dancer Shearer
52 Arctic
53 Miss __ of "Dallas"
55 Sandy ridge
58 Best or Ferber
60 Trademark
61 Memorable periods
62 Force unit
65 "Leave __ to
Heaven"

ACROSS

1 Zsa Zsa, e.g.
6 Game of no chance
10 Canadian Indian
14 Better than
15 Christmas pageant prop
16 Auditorium
17 Quick
18 Served perfectly on a court
19 "Hallelujah! I'm __"
20 Carnival fun for some
23 Part
24 Glider section
25 Speed up
29 Columnist Landers
30 Kind of sax
31 Pianist Templeton
34 Shapeless forms of matter
39 Thoroughly
42 Play a banjo
43 Norman city
44 Discovery's agcy.
45 Cry of delight
47 Mickey creator
49 Near
53 Fruit of the __
55 Diplomatic officer
61 Seamstress Betsy
62 Lobster tail, to a diner
63 Orchard
64 Words of relativity
65 Except
66 Bit of burning coal
67 Rusk or Martin
68 Winged
69 Rapier's big brother

DOWN

1 Barbed spear
2 Competent
3 Afrikaner
4 Ended
5 Head for bed
6 Serape, e.g.
7 Hide the loot
8 Sheltered, at sea
9 Up-to-date
10 Garden green
11 Fanatical
12 Avoid
13 Lewis's Gantry
21 Sub finder
22 Sudden thrust
25 Stetsons or shakos
26 Very much
27 Marshal's badge
28 Bean-curd product
29 Yearning
32 Labor leader Walesa
33 Airline abbr.
35 Barley bristles

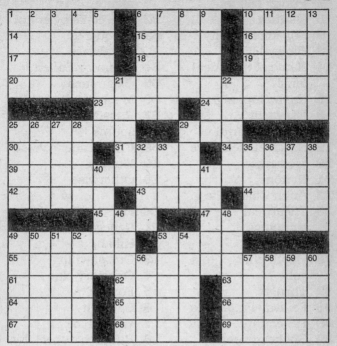

94

36 Actor Connery
37 In addition
38 Highly amuse: Colloq.
40 Surrounded by
41 "Till the __ Time"
46 Ukranian seaport
48 Reflections
49 Stinging
50 "__ were the days"

51 "__ luego"
52 Criminal act
53 Polliwog, for one
54 Present
56 Twofold
57 Role for Shirley or Marie
58 Charles or Lynda Bird
59 Perpetually
60 Dried up

ACROSS

1 Funny fellows
5 Quahog
9 Phoenician deity
13 Biblical land
14 Name of theatrical fame
15 Nacho topping
16 Easy gait
17 Collier's portal
18 Nautical measures
19 Mollusks
21 Notions
22 Anna Christie, e.g.
23 Theatrical trappings
25 Novice
28 Depth charge, to a gob
32 Thrusts
36 Fenway Pk. judges
38 Pa. county
39 Shakespearean villain
40 Quick
41 Pollux's mother
42 Ancient Syria
43 Marathon segments
44 Pellucid
45 Mib
47 Aleutian island
49 Cream __
51 P.L.O. leader
56 Triple Crown horse: 1935

59 Kin of three card monte
62 Overcome by ennui
63 Lacquered metalware
64 Opera by Salieri
65 Calamities
66 Muscat sultanate
67 Russian news source
68 Cheerleader's verse
69 Flat fee
70 Otherwise

DOWN

1 Renege on a wager
2 Hilo hi
3 One yawning
4 Olfactory clue
5 Foxlike
6 Calif. city
7 W.W. II foe
8 Bulfinch's specialty
9 Concert site
10 Medicinal plant
11 The Charleses' pooch
12 Bonnie young girl
15 Revue segments
20 Building sites
24 Cardinal point
26 Be kinglike
27 Last letter from Greece
29 Algonquian Indian
30 Rival of Amneris

95

31 Stingy
32 Thailand, formerly
33 "G.W.T.W." survivor
34 Culture medium
35 Epithet for some Hollywood blondes
37 Nuisance
40 Skedaddled
44 Weightlifter's exercise
46 Cargoes

48 __ scout
50 John Jacob __
52 Variegated quartz
53 Deadly
54 Bring together
55 Concise
56 Mind
57 Chess action
58 Seed jacket
60 Kind of plate
61 Joie de vivre

ACROSS

1 __ mater
5 Prayer at a meal
10 Spa in England
14 Froth
15 Assistants
16 Monster
17 160 square rods
18 "The __ Menagerie": Williams
19 Bar order
20 Restaurateur Leonard Slye
22 "The __ Musketeers"
23 Currier and __
24 Earth: Comb. form
26 Separated
29 A tempest in a __
32 Boston airport
33 Slender
35 Heroic poem
37 Wing for Amor
38 Grave
41 Dockworkers' org.
42 Fluent
44 Curse
45 Pitch pipe, e.g.
47 Slept noisily
49 Covers walls, e.g.
50 Eat out
51 African chief
52 Performed
55 Actress Alexandra Zuck

60 Portal
61 Glowing coal
62 Cultivate
63 Bancroft or Baxter
64 Area under a pitched roof
65 Gabor and Tanguay
66 Humble
67 Midges
68 Victor Borge, e.g.

DOWN

1 At a distance
2 Crazy
3 Astor or Martin
4 "God Bless __"
5 Choked
6 Gets one's goat
7 Jewish month
8 Stop
9 Tee predecessor
10 Boxer Packy East
11 Ripening agent
12 Elm or fir
13 Present
21 Baking chambers
22 __-la-la
25 Knee
26 Dross
27 Counts heads
28 Encore!
30 Think

96

31 Roofer,
sometimes
33 Artisan
34 Homophone for
hymn
36 Freeway sights
39 Paradise
40 Single step
43 Actress Cathleen
Collins
46 Modernized
48 Disencumber

49 Spanish priests
51 Prepared to be
knighted
52 Rib donor
53 Ice-cream holder
54 Musical sound
56 Eastern bishop's
title
57 Prima donna
58 Verve
59 Other
61 Roe

ACROSS

1 Tweed was one
5 "M*A*S*H" role
10 King of humor
14 Touch upon
15 Sidestep
16 One of the Youngers
17 Chesterfield
18 Popular politician
20 Bulk
21 Flock mom
22 Built
23 Builds
25 Egyptian deity
26 Banquets
28 Support
33 Work unit
34 Modern chair designer
36 Provocative
37 Missing a suit, in bridge
39 Hire
41 Hersholt or Harlow
42 Four-door flop
44 Kind of theater
46 __-Magnon
47 Abjures
49 Followed a regimen
51 Turndown
52 Old Italian coin
53 Legal move
57 Letter opener
58 Tabriz is here
61 Hopefuls at the polls
63 O. Henry product
64 Gray of "Buck Rogers"
65 The Four Hundred
66 Siouan of Okla.
67 Actress Wynter
68 Seen less
69 English horn, e.g.

DOWN

1 Blowout
2 Hautboy
3 Woodhull or Pankhurst
4 Union members
5 Setback
6 Promises
7 Prom partner
8 Humorist George
9 Rue
10 "The Frogs" kickoff, e.g.
11 Real estate
12 Helmsman's call
13 Wimp's cousin
19 Vanderbilt Cup seats
24 Gormandized
25 Henry on trumpet
26 High excitement
27 Diminish
28 Chicago eleven
29 British rule in India

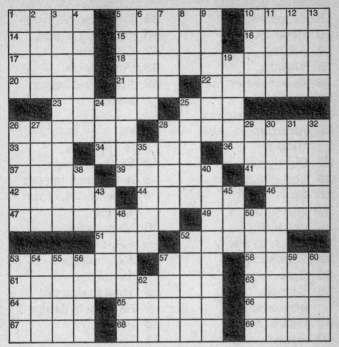

97

30 Targets of
  61 Across
31 Be rude, in a way
32 Ecclesiastical
  assembly
35 Substantial
38 "_ Rosenkavalier"
40 Nominee's
  important
  supporter
43 Veranda
45 Trouble

48 Modern sculptor
50 Masthead entry
52 Nueve menos
  dos
53 Served a winner
54 Brazilian river
55 Nabokov opus
56 Poet Millay
57 Hullabaloo
59 S. African lily
60 Hunger for
62 Tenn. neighbor

ACROSS

1 Make up yarns
5 Score settler
10 Hops drier
14 Inkling
15 Vibrant
16 Home of the Jazz
17 Up against it
19 Soybean product
20 Affliction
21 "Righto!"
22 Slowly seeped
23 Leave high and dry
25 Guy
27 Josephine of mysteries
28 Knits, in a way
32 Winds around
35 Gate
38 Give the old heave-ho
39 Part of A.D.
40 Adds punch to the punch
41 __ Major
42 Pianist Peter
43 Conestoga team
44 Scoff
45 Engages completely
47 Airport abbr.
48 Follow
51 Gear for cowboys
55 Coincide
58 Makeup mishap
60 Arles assent
61 Countenance
62 Thwarts
64 Gung-ho
65 Type size
66 Cheering words
67 Coop group
68 Some votes
69 Flaunting bogus taste

DOWN

1 Is apparent
2 Vinitera grape
3 Act or lock opener
4 This word has no vowels
5 Mimic's forte
6 Slept like __
7 Exclamations of dismay
8 Turn inside out
9 Musical syllables
10 Prohibited
11 From __ (completely)
12 Diamond call
13 Flump's cousin
18 Shore fliers
22 Birds __ feather
24 In an unsettled state
26 Freezes
29 Beguile
30 Being, to a philosopher
31 Betelgeuse, e.g.
32 Lingo

98

33 "The __ Love": 1924 song

34 Concerning

35 Weigh heavily on

36 Good thing to have in a hole

37 Author Kesey

40 Prunes

44 Bart or Belle

46 An article, in Arles

47 Delights

49 Customary choice of words

50 Samms and Lazarus

52 Sub-finding device

53 Zero

54 Actress Spacek

55 Nanking nanny

56 Be generous

57 Restrain

59 Italian name of note

62 __ fever

63 Author Levin

ACROSS

1 Goodbye, in Grenoble
6 Literary collection
9 Suppress
14 Turner and Cantrell
15 European cap
16 Wed
17 Imports
18 Unit of electrical resistance
19 Lolls
20 Perfume ingredient
21 Southern group of stars
22 Revision of 20 Across
23 Tatum's dad
24 Crank
26 Jane of fiction
27 Enticed
29 Diner sign
31 Pup, at times
33 Absorbed, in a way
37 Poetic conjunction
38 Handful
40 Polloi preceder
41 Pork __ (picnic dish)
43 Poplar varieties
45 Sicilian spouter
46 __ a million
47 Dept. helper
50 Biblical land
52 Wax: Sp.
55 An anagram for 20 Across
57 Sometimes it's smelled
58 Letter opener
59 Musical endings
60 Former ring king
61 Prod
62 Gives thumbs up
63 Mine, in Milano
64 City on the Rhone
65 Edgy
66 D.C. figure
67 Equals

DOWN

1 Creator of Phil the Fiddler
2 Oxeye
3 Performed an Inauguration Day rite
4 Devoured completely
5 Largest land, once
6 "All __!"
7 Indira Gandhi's father
8 Military ware
9 Cease
10 Get ready for bed
11 Choreographer Alvin __
12 Revision of 20 Across
13 "Steppenwolf" author
24 Pertinent
25 Exhibition

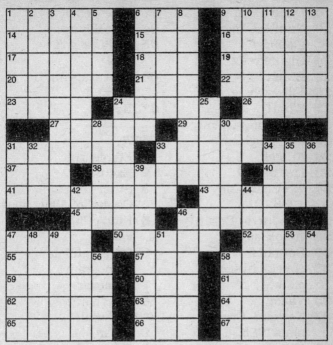

28 Revision of 20 Across
30 Revision of 20 Across
31 Affirmative
32 Feathered fisher
33 "__ Over," Orbison song
34 "Eye of __," Follett novel
35 Long time
36 Roman underworld god
39 This puzzle's theme

42 Gives away, in a way
44 Envision
46 Choice
47 Scarf
48 Stir the fire
49 Car or chair
51 Cantab's rival
53 Angry person
54 In __ (tousled)
56 To live, to Livy
58 Cinch

ACROSS

1 Bygone days
5 Dried plum
10 Numbers men, for short
14 High: Prefix
15 Bitter
16 Killer whale
17 Wharf
18 Declaims violently
19 Optical glass
20 Rub off
22 Lies at rest
24 First lady, May 7, 1988?
27 Conductor Dorati
28 Heroic story
30 Bounder
33 Greek physician of note
35 Valley
37 Newman-Cruise film: 1986
41 Fair
42 Parrots' pates
43 Letter before aitch
44 From afar: Comb. form
46 Bell sound
48 Flag bearer
54 Tell
56 Lengthier
57 King of Norway
58 Dutch city, with "The"
61 Challenge
62 In __ (in position)
63 Blue-pencils
64 A deadly sin
65 Achilles' soft spot
66 Descartes and Coty
67 Beams

DOWN

1 Edible fruit
2 Excuse
3 Strict
4 Capital of Albania
5 Kind of home or leave
6 Corporate monogram
7 Samovar
8 Peterman's material
9 A Ford
10 Centennial State
11 Shanghaiers' kin
12 Teen-age skin problem
13 Lip
21 Australian wild dog
23 Opposite of neg.
25 Lively round dance
26 Small-sized reading glasses
29 Toward shelter

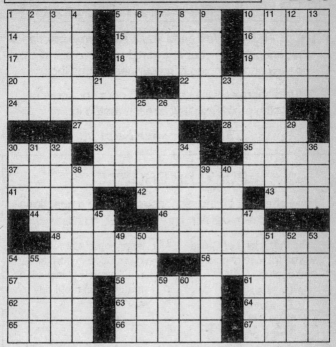

30 Pennies: Abbr.

31 "Cat on __ Tin Roof"

32 Profane

34 __ prosequi

36 Regard

38 Vivid

39 Intrepid

40 Tropical fruit

45 Guido's high note

47 Kind of gap

49 Different

50 Aptly named novelist

51 Capital of Guam

52 Brazen

53 Low cards

54 Snack

55 "I cannot tell __"

59 Type of rummy

60 Shoshonean

Help us puzzle you better and get . . .

| ¹F | R | E | E | | ²P | U | Z | Z | L | E | S |

!

That's right! We'll send you a set of **free** puzzles—
just for checking off your answers to the two questions
below and dropping it in your nearest mailbox.

Your responses will enable us to offer you more of
the puzzles that you're interested in.

Thanks for your help!

PUZZLER PROFILE

I have checked off my responses to the two questions
below. Please send me my FREE puzzles!

1. I like these kind of Cross-
   words (please check all
   that apply):
   __ Daily-size
   __ Sunday-size
   __ Very difficult
   __ Large-print
   __ Acrostics (quotations)
   __ Cryptics (British-style)
   __ Variety word games
   (Like those in GAMES and
   other puzzle magazines.)

2. Approximate number of
   puzzle books from all
   publishers (not including
   magazines) that I buy
   each year:
   __ 1 to 2
   __ 3 to 5
   __ 6 to 10
   __ 11 or more

NAME_____

ADDRESS_____

CITY_____STATE_____ZIP_____

SEND TO: **PUZZLER PROFILE**
                P.O. BOX 124
                MEDFORD, NY 11763

SOLUTIONS

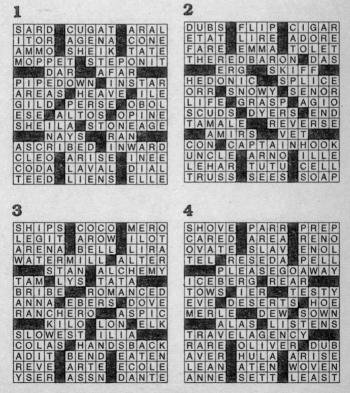

1

S	A	R	D		C	U	G	A	T		A	R	A	L
I	T	O	R		A	G	E	N	A		C	O	N	E
A	M	M	O		S	H	E	I	K		T	A	T	E
M	O	P	P	E	T		S	T	E	P	O	N	I	T
			D	A	R			A	F	A	R			
P	I	P	E	D	O	W	N		I	N	S	T	A	R
A	R	E	A	S		H	E	A	V	E		I	L	E
G	I	L	D		P	E	R	S	E		O	B	O	L
E	S	E		A	L	T	O	S		O	P	I	N	E
S	H	E	I	L	A		S	T	O	N	E	A	G	E
			N	A	Y	S			R	A	N			
A	S	C	R	I	B	E	D		I	N	W	A	R	D
C	L	E	O		A	R	I	S	E		I	N	E	E
C	O	D	A		L	A	V	A	L		D	I	A	L
T	E	E	D		L	I	E	N	S		E	L	L	E

2

D	U	B	S		F	L	I	P		C	I	G	A	R
E	T	A	T		L	I	R	E		A	D	O	R	E
F	A	R	E		E	M	M	A		T	O	L	E	T
T	H	E	R	E	D	B	A	R	O	N		D	A	S
				E	R	G			S	K	I	F	F	
H	E	D	O	N	I	C		S	P	L	I	C	E	
O	R	R		S	N	O	W	Y		S	E	N	O	R
L	I	F	E		G	R	A	S	P		A	G	I	O
S	C	U	D	S		D	Y	E	R	S		E	N	D
T	A	M	A	L	E		R	E	V	E	R	S	E	
			A	M	I	R	S		V	E	T			
C	O	N		C	A	P	T	A	I	N	H	O	O	K
U	N	C	L	E		A	R	N	O		I	L	L	E
L	E	H	A	R		T	U	T	U		C	E	L	L
T	R	U	S	S		S	E	E	S		S	O	A	P

3

S	H	I	P	S		C	O	C	O		M	E	R	O
L	E	G	I	T		A	R	O	W		I	L	O	T
A	R	E	N	A		B	E	L	L		L	I	R	A
W	A	T	E	R	M	I	L	L		A	L	T	E	R
			S	T	A	N		A	L	C	H	E	M	Y
T	A	M		L	Y	S		T	A	T	A			
B	R	I	B	E		R	O	M	A	N	C	E	D	
A	N	N	A		E	B	E	R	S		D	O	V	E
R	A	N	C	H	E	R	O		A	S	P	I	C	
			K	I	L	O		L	O	N		E	L	K
S	L	O	W	E	S	T		I	L	I	A			
C	O	L	A	S		H	A	N	D	S	B	A	C	K
A	D	I	T		B	E	N	D		E	A	T	E	N
R	E	V	E		A	R	T	E		E	C	O	L	E
Y	S	E	R		A	S	S	N		D	A	N	T	E

4

S	H	O	V	E		P	A	R	R		P	R	E	P
C	A	R	E	D		A	R	E	A		R	E	N	O
O	V	A	T	E		S	L	A	V		E	N	O	L
T	E	L		R	E	S	E	D	A		P	E	L	L
			P	L	E	A	S	E	G	O	A	W	A	Y
I	C	E	B	E	R	G		R	E	A	R			
T	O	W	S		I	E	R		T	E	S	T	Y	
E	V	E		D	E	S	E	R	T	S		H	O	E
M	E	R	L	E		D	E	W		S	O	W	N	
			A	L	A	S		L	I	S	T	E	N	S
T	R	A	V	E	L	A	G	E	N	C	Y			
R	A	R	E		O	L	I	V	E	R		D	U	B
A	V	E	R		H	U	L	A		A	R	I	S	E
L	E	A	N		A	T	E	N		W	O	V	E	N
A	N	N	E		S	E	T	T		L	E	A	S	T

5

```
S L A G   F L A T S   A P I S
W I P E   R O S I E   W O N T
A D E N   O C T E T   L O D E
B O X E R S H O R T S   D I E
      V A T   S E C U L A R
V O C A T I O N   E A S E
A S H   S E D A N   R E C A P
S L O E   R E D I D   D U P E
T O W N S   S I N E W   T I E
    H O E S   R E P R I S A L
C L O S E T S   L I N
A A U   P A C E S E T T E R S
P U N T   C O R O T   O K I E
E D D A   K N I F E   N E V A
R E S T   S E C T S   E D E N
```

6

```
L A I D   A G U E   S P I T
I S L E   L A N D S   P O S E
S H O E P O L I S H   A L E A
      P A T E N   E S T E R S
O P E N   S T R A P   V E E
S P O R T Y   E U R E K A
E E L   Y A W N S   W O U L D
T R I O   M E T E R   P L A Y
S A S S Y   N I S U S   T R E
    H A I R D O   B L E E D S
D I E   P A Y N E   A I D S
U N D O E S   A V A S T
A D O G   P O L I S H H A M S
L I F E   S A L T S   E D I T
S A F E   R Y A N   R O S Y
```

7

```
J I L T S   B R A   B O R E
A D O R E   W R I T   E V E N
P O W E R H O U S E   C E N T
E L S A   E R N E S   A R T E
      T E R S E   T E M P E R
A P S I S   E T A   L E O
R O U S T S   I R E   W E D
A P P E A L S   R I V I E R A
B E E   T Y R   B E D R I D
    R Y E   O C S   N E S T S
R I P E S T   L A S S O
A M O S   A B A S H   L E D A
Y A W S   H O R S E P O W E R
O G E E   O B E Y   A G E N T
N E R D   E S T   L Y R E S
```

8

```
A S C A P   E D A M   F A C T
S T A T E   V E R A   A L O E
A A R O N   A T A N   L I R E
D R O P P E D E G G   L E O N
      A M E N   E V E N T S
B R I D L E   T U R I N
L E N O   R E E S   E A G L E
E N D W A Y S   E N T R E A T
D O O N E   T E R A   C O T T
    G R E E N   D A H L I A
M A T R O N   T A I L
A G R A   L O W E R W O R L D
T O E D   I B I D   A V O I R
E R N E   S O N E   Y A L T A
D A D S   T E E S   S L E E T
```

9

```
C L A M P   H A H A   C A F E
R A D I I   E L A N   L U L L
T I A R A   L A I N   I T E M
  C R A Z Y L I K E A F O X
      Z O O   A L F
N A S S A U   C U L L   S P T
O D A L   N E L L   O T T E R
R E M I N G T O N S T E E L E
S P O D E   O V A L   A R T S
E T A   G E N E   A S S E S S
    E R R   A P T
  S I M O N A N D S I M O N
T Y R O   I R I D   G A L A S
A N A T   E C C E   M I A M I
R E N E   S H E D   A N N E X
```

10

```
A S T A   S H A M S   A C E S
B O I L   T E N E T   S O S O
C O M E D O W N T O E A R T H
S T E R E O   E A R N   N E O
      T A D S   L E T T
H I P   N O T A   S E R A P H
O L L A   U R S A   T E P E E
P L A N E T O F T H E A P E S
E A T E R   P A S O   T A V S
S T E A M S   R E U P   L E E
    R I T A   A N E W
R O E   N O V A   D R A G E E
A S T H E W O R L D T U R N S
F L O E   E I E I O   G A I N
T O N Y   D R A N G   H Y D E
```

11

```
PARLE_BACH_JAW
OBOES_ORTHO_OLE
ABAFT_PERIL_SOB
CELTICTWILIGHT_
HYD_MOS_DER____
___LAG_PERSEIDS
SENAT_SERE_GRIT
THEWESTERNWORLD
EROS_PUNS_ORALS
MENUHINS_PRY___
_ION_AGR_SAE
ARTISTASAYOUNG
AGA_STALK_INANE
FEZ_TERMS_NEVIS
TEE_SRTA_GREET
```

12

```
PAPA_BERG_CLAM
IGOR_SOLAR_RAGE
LOGE_PLANE_IMRE
EGO_ALUMINUMBAT
_SALAS_AVE_
RATIFY_MADEAHIT
ACIDS_CANEA_ADA
DOCS_SORTS_MMLII
IRK_ATONE_WOMEN
ONSTRIKE_COVERT
_ELF_RAWER_
FIVEOFCLUBS_HEM
ADAM_ERODE_DELI
NONE_NEVER_EASE
SLED_SEER_EDEN
```

13

```
BALKS_CASH_TONK
AGAIN_ALEA_ANON
TRONA_CLAN_KENE
HANDTOHAND_ENCE
_HUEY_ELIDES
SACHET_ELLEN_
ALLA_DODO_SHARE
STENTOR_UNTAMED
HOWDY_ESTA_NINE
_IRISH_SUDDEN
LLANOS_ELAN_
OUCH_ONALLHANDS
ACTA_BARA_APART
TION_ANEM_NEPAL
HAND_RARA_DRAGO
```

14

```
PSAT_MOO_ASSAY
UMBO_AILS_PHASE
LEON_GNAT_PERON
ELL_CLOVERLEAFS
SLIPPER_NUIT_
_SEAT_ASSESSED
ASHES_EMITS_ARI
RAIL_PRIVY_SNIP
ANN_SAUCE_GATES
LAGNAPPE_MATA_
_ANET_POLECAT
SEMIDRIVERS_LIE
UTILE_OARS_MAME
PACER_NIKE_IRAN
SLEDS_SNY_GATS
```

15

```
DISC_LEAKS_MAMA
INCA_ATRIP_IMAN
EGAN_STOLA_DINT
TOPOTHEMORNIN_
STENO_ASTO_OOH
_EBB_ARCADE
LEI_ALOE_MACED
CENTEROFGRAVITY
ANSEL_WAGE_EDS
STEREO_SOL_
TOM_CADS_OASTS
_BOTTOMLESSPIT
GOLD_ERIES_TITO
ACED_RITAS_ORAN
PASS_SCENE_RENE
```

16

```
POSSE_NOIR_TOME
ETHEL_INCA_ALAR
CHINESECHECKERS
KON_VOLE_HEAVE
_RAIL_TAUT_
SCOTTISHBROGUE
ROUSE_PEEL_ANS
INRE_PLANT_OMIT
MAI_SEAN_ACUTE
ARABIANKNIGHTS
_ORLE_ADES_
AMORE_ABEL_CRY
JAPANESEBEETLES
ANAT_SORE_SAUTE
ROLE_PLOD_SPEER
```

17

```
GALL   NASA   HARP
ALIAS  ISIS   AWOL
STORK  GIGI   NATO
HANDINHAND   DROP
     RAT   ELMER
SPELLS  FUSEE
URGE   ALAN   ADOPT
MOAN   LETIT  OLIO
PADDY  FETE   WELL
   SALTS   TANGLE
  SHAKE    JON
SHAH   SECONDHAND
LAVA   SARI   EERIE
ADEN   OVEN   SMILE
VEND   NEWT   SLED
```

18

```
CRAB   REARM   TWO
RAIL   HOLLOA  HOW
UNDERACLOUD    URN
SKEWER   GERUNDS
     ONES    SOLD
MAUVE  QED   NEEDS
OLPE   TUXEDO  REL
VAIR   HAILS   HILO
INN    VELLUM  ENVY
ESTEE  LEG   PAGED
   HONE    ELEV
EVENING   ATEASE
LEA    STORMCENTER
SRI    ORDERS  LEAN
EAR    NESTS   YENS
```

19

```
SAWN    SORA    WEIR
ONEI   OCTET   ELMO
DISC   NORTHWALES
ALTE   ETO   ERRATA
   INSET    MNO
SANELY   DISTRESS
ODD    YEMEN   HEATH
FAIR   DEMON   ASIA
ANETS  DATES   TEL
ROSETTES   WIDEST
   AES    ASTOR
ODESSA  RIM   ETAL
SOUTHSHORE   SIDE
LURE   EATEN   IDES
ODOM   SPED    NENE
```

20

```
ABEAD   QUAG   ACT
TERRA   URSA   GARP
HANKYPANKY    OMER
ETE    SIS   AROMA
NEST   NAMBYPAMBY
ARTEL  RAISE   ILE
   AID   RLS   SLED
HELTERSKELTER
NONE   MAH   LEE
EMS    RONAS   TAPIR
WILLYNILLY    DINO
ALAIN   ORE    ETA
RIVE   HOCUSPOCUS
KEEN   ERIC   EVENT
SDS    MOTH   EASES
```

21

```
SHOP   CHAR   ACTED
KERR   HOLE   VOILE
IRAE   OBIE   OSCAN
MATTEROFFACT
STEELE   SEAMEW
   NEST   CITRATE
SPASM  HOOD    CUL
TAKEITORLEAVEIT
ANE    ALTO   MISSY
TINWARE   ROIS
OCEANS    ASCEND
   POINTOFHONOR
GELID  ASTI   UNTO
OVATE  PAIS   NEAP
TAXIS  ARCH   TASS
```

22

```
WAND   SEDER   SOAR
ALOE   ALIVE   TAME
GIST   DEVASTATED
   THECAVANAUGHS
   NOTE    LIE
STATES   CHESSMAN
PILED  CHASM   ONA
AMOS   AAR    BUNK
CON    BASIE  DONEE
ENGRAVER   LAUDED
   ANI    WONG
BARNARDHUGHES
REGISTERED    TRIM
CART   ENURE   UNDO
ADAY   SOBER   PEEP
```

23

```
LARAS RITA  ANDA
AGENT ADEN  QUES
MANSE VEND  URNS
BROWNIE  TRIESTE
   ETONS  OLDEST
PARROT  ADIEU
ATO RAFTED  CLAP
CLAWS AIM  ATONE
TINA FIRSTS  NNW
  INURE  OSAGES
CARTER  SURER
AMIABLE  BOSSUET
BOOB OLIO  SINCE
ALTI NASA  ONICE
LEST GNAT  RETEM
```

24

```
SWAB GAITS  COAT
TARA OUTRE  OLGA
AVID ONSET  NEAR
REALIST  POPCORN
   USE  DANSE
TOUCHDOWN  HAULS
HUNK ORE  CALLUP
ENS SWALLOW  TRI
ICEMAN LOU  PRIN
RERAN  DOWNGRADE
   RESIN  TOO
SIERRAS  ADDRESS
ASTI CHARO  ARLO
METE RENEW  TMAN
SEED ESTAN  EATS
```

25

```
CAKE SOAP  AGATE
AMOS INGE  COLON
PURPLECOW  CLOUD
ESE OSE  ELUDERS
TEAPOT  REESE
  INANE  VENDOR
SHONE EDDY  GORE
PERKY ALI  TOMES
TRAP DLIV  ROOST
SOLACE  OASIS
  NOLAN  ALETTE
SMOTHER AIL  ORA
PECHE  YELLOWDOG
ESTER ARGO  HAVE
CHORE NEAR  OYER
```

26

```
MODUS CHAR  PESO
ABUSE HUGE  ICER
POKER ORAL  ARAD
SEE  PHILRIZZUTO
  SHEAR  SEZ
AWNING  REHEARD
WRIST CUKES  ORG
LIDS FLIES  AGEE
STE GLAND  CLEAT
ERELONG  BOARDS
  DEW  PURIM
PEEWEEREESE  AMI
ALDA RONA  TIRED
LEER EMIL  TRITE
LEND DADS  ASSES
```

27

```
ARAG ASPIC  ALMA
NOTE CEARA  SEAS
NATO  ERNIEBANKS
ARARAT SSE  TEN
  GLAD  HADJ
CREATOR  REOPEN
CHUB ENOL  WHERE
HEIR SONIC  NARD
ARNEL RAMA  NCOS
STATUS  SPRAYER
  TINA  SERB
ALS GEM  STELLA
WILLIEMAYS  NOEL
ARIA RANEE  CRAM
YAMS SNAPS  HENS
```

28

```
TINA ADAGE  BAKU
ARAM RULES  EGIS
SOVIETCOMPOSERS
SNY MUTES  AESIR
  FER  ESE
IGORSTRAVINSKY
IVORY HARES  HIE
GALA BATON  KARL
ONE SONIA  SOKOL
RIMSKYKORSAKOV
  IAD  IDO
TAUNT SPUNK  RBL
SERGEIPROKOFIEV
ARAL NAOMI  ALLO
ROLE ANTON  SLAV
```

29

```
GAMER AJAR WHEY
OLIVE RIFE YALE
LAMIA EGIS EMMA
DRILLMASTER MET
    MESA LASERS
BEHEST WELDER
OLAX EASY ITHAD
BITTERN CHISELS
SACRA ILKA TALC
  HASSLE WOODYS
FIESTA VEER
ART SCREWDRIVER
RAJA KALE EDILE
ETON EVER REESE
DEBT DIRS YAWED
```

30

```
SCAB RADII SWAT
LOGO EVANS TINE
ALEX MARIONETTE
MERCHANT BEATEN
    AINT FARM
SPARED MARVELED
PAN DECOR ERICA
ASES RAREE SKAT
SHAME NORMA ERE
MARATHON PLANTS
    RHEE ELAN
COSTAR IRONCLAD
PLAINASDAY HILO
ALME LOOSE OVEN
SAPS DOLED REST
```

31

```
SGT OHARA SKIP
AREA BISON TONE
KISSMEKATE IONA
INTHERED MONKS
   MOD CONGA
TAKEON CANDYBAR
AWAY RAREE UGH
TARE POKES TRAY
UKE TAPED GRIM
MENDERES OCTANE
  BRAID AKA
SLIMS SNAPPISH
MOAN HANKYPANKY
LUCK EDILE RAYE
IRKS SATED TER
```

32

```
CLACK SCAM BARE
ROGUE ARCA ELIA
APART BATT LENT
BELLTHECAT LUGE
    LARK EMPTOR
BIGBEN ENDUE
AMIE SARI SPELT
BELLMAN STEPTOE
ATALE APIA EARN
  WASTE PARSED
COGENT NOEL
ABET RINGSABELL
MESH ORAL SOTIE
ESTE LANE KOREA
LEER LETS AMEND
```

33

```
GELS STEAD STEP
AVOW TANGO LAVA
ZEROMOSTEL OXEN
ANDREWS EMPIRE
   DTS FDA
CENSE EEL CATER
ORO INDICATIVE
NOTHINGINCOMMON
ASCENDANTS EKE
NEHRU GAS SCREW
   RAE OER
SHAKEN SWEATER
LONI GROUNDZERO
OATS LORRE ELIA
EXES EDGED DEEM
```

34

```
DUPE PASSE BEAR
OPAL ORIEL ERLE
ROCKSTARWINWOOD
ANT PALES EASES
   SIS HAI
PITCHERCARLTON
CANOE TEARS ONO
ORCA CHARD KNIT
PTA SIETE DEICE
SINGERLAWRENCE
   ARE ENT
OHARA COAST BAA
COMICLANDESBERG
TRES ARMEN ALEE
SASH SPENT GLAD
```

35

```
SHORT ACTS  TODD
TIBER TRAP  APER
ALONE TINE  GATE
GOLDBRICKER  LES
    LOCK  DOWERS
ADDLES  ENSUES
FOIE SATE  SACRE
TRANSIT  ENTREAT
SAMOA TERI  ONIT
 ORDEAL  GENTLE
 VENEER  EYES
ODD  SILVERSMITH
TILT CUES  ELSIE
ELIA ANNE  NILES
DELE SASS  EVERS
```

36

```
ROAD SCAM  BLUNT
OGLE TAPA  AIRED
ORES OMER  SODAS
KEEPONESCHINUP
   OLEO   ONE
LASTED  CRUELLER
ANTI BOOST  ARE
STICKTOONESGUNS
EAR LOLLS  ADIT
RESPONDS  PARSES
  ONT  PEAG
 HOLDONESGROUND
TORII ETAT  YSER
ABACK STLO  LEDA
DONEE SUMP  ERST
```

37

```
TRAY FLIP  GIBB
WAKE TRADE  ONEE
ITISAWORLDTOSEE
TEN MISSY  ODONT
   COST  SPA
POVERTYISNOSIN
OPEN NOEL  SAY
KENT PULSE  ALDA
ERA SOLE  PAIR
 ALLPOETSAREMAD
  EAR  TOAD
ANENT SMART  ARK
WARISACONTAGION
EMIT TOSCA  ANTE
DENY ETTE  STEW
```

38

```
WADE MAHAL  MCCC
OVAL EBONY  OHOH
RENE GOWER  TRUE
TRACYAUSTIN  IRS
  TONTO  COASTS
ARBOR   AIMEE
NOIRE  CONSERVED
ELL CAROM  ESO
WELLLIKED  HERTZ
 IRONY  ONTHE
OREGON  BEING
TAJ  NAVRATILOVA
HIED MEARA  ICED
ESAU ORIEL  STIR
RANG NEDDY  HANA
```

39

```
BASS LETUP  EDNA
OLLA ORONO  TROT
STILLWATER  HIRT
NEPALESE  CHANDU
  DARE  THINK
ASTON RAH  NEWER
MARION LOST  AVE
AXEL OPERA  PTAS
ZOA AMOR  TALENT
ENDED ETH  TERSE
 WRIST  ELLA
SPARTA  TREASURE
IOTA SHEARWATER
GLEN HELLO  NATS
HERD ALADY  THEE
```

40

```
AMAH DARN  TSARS
LATE ELIA  ITCHY
ASEA SINS  LEMON
SHERLOCKHOLMES
  TETE   RES
FALLTO AFAR  ELS
ADIEU SNIT  OLEA
THESPECKLEDBAND
SONS VALE  OSTIA
OCS TIRE  LUCENT
  NUT  TABU
 THEBAKERSTREET
SHAVE IRIS  IDLE
OUTER WINE  NEBS
USERS ICES  GNAT
```

41

A	F	A	R		A	R	O	M	A		H	E	R	B
L	O	S	E		R	A	M	O	N		A	X	E	L
E	X	A	S	P	E	R	A	T	E		Z	A	M	A
E	X	P	O	R	T	E	R		S	P	I	G	O	T
			N	O	E	L		S	T	I	N	G		
O	C	E	A	N		Y	A	P		A	G	E	O	F
S	E	X	T	E	T		R	O	L	F		R	U	E
A	S	H	E		E	L	I	T	E		S	A	T	E
K	A	I		A	L	A	S		G	R	A	T	E	D
A	R	L	E	S		N	E	G		E	W	E	R	S
		A	L	I	C	E		L	E	A	H			
U	P	R	O	A	R		P	A	N	D	O	R	A	S
R	E	A	P		E	X	E	N	T	E	R	A	T	E
A	R	T	E		M	I	N	C	E		S	I	T	E
L	I	E	D		E	I	D	E	R		E	L	A	N

42

S	A	F	E	R		A	L	M	S		S	C	A	T
A	W	A	R	E		M	E	D	E		P	O	U	R
C	O	U	R	T	L	I	E	S	T		L	U	N	A
R	L	S		R	I	S	K		T	H	I	R	T	Y
E	S	T	E	E	M		S	E	L	E	C	T		
			S	A	N	D		D	E	F	E	R	S	
E	L	A	N	D		I	N	E	R	T		O	A	R
L	O	G	E		S	L	I	M	S		M	O	V	E
S	K	I		S	C	A	L	A		T	I	M	E	D
	I	N	P	A	R	T		S	P	O	T			
		C	O	P	I	E	S		O	N	E	M	A	N
E	G	O	I	S	M		A	I	L	S		A	C	E
P	I	U	S		P	A	Y	C	O	U	R	T	T	O
I	N	R	E		E	L	S	E		R	A	T	O	N
C	A	T	S		D	I	O	R		E	W	E	R	S

43

S	H	A	R	P		F	O	L	D		S	T	A	R
E	A	G	E	R		O	B	I	E		E	R	I	E
T	R	A	P	E	Z	O	I	D	S		G	E	N	T
S	P	Y		J	O	L	T		E	Q	U	A	T	E
			P	U	N	S		T	R	U	E	D		
A	R	C	A	D	E		N	O	V	A		M	A	T
T	H	O	N	G		G	O	R	E	N		I	S	H
T	O	T	E	M		U	T	E		T	U	L	S	A
A	N	T		E	B	S	E	N		I	N	L	A	W
R	E	E		N	E	T	S		S	T	A	S	I	S
		R	A	T	S	O		A	L	A	S			
A	P	P	O	S	E		U	N	I	T		B	O	A
L	A	I	R		E	X	P	E	D	I	T	I	N	G
T	I	N	T		C	I	O	N		V	I	N	C	E
E	L	S	A		H	I	N	T		E	N	D	E	D

44

G	O	L	D		R	O	S	S		A	R	I	L	T
E	R	I	E		A	N	E	T		T	A	N	Y	A
E	L	E	C	T	I	O	N	R	E	T	U	R	N	S
R	E	S	O	W	S		N	A	S	A		E	N	S
			R	E	E		A	P	S	I	S			
C	O	S		E	D	E		E	N	C	A	G	E	
A	R	C	E	D		T	E	E	N		O	R	R	S
P	A	R	T	Y	C	O	N	V	E	N	T	I	O	N
E	T	A	H		A	N	T	E		O	S	A	G	E
	S	E	P	I	A	S		N	U	N		S	S	S
			C	L	A	R	A		S	A	E			
A	T	M		B	L	A	B		E	G	R	E	T	S
T	H	O	M	A	S	J	E	F	F	E	R	S	O	N
T	A	R	O	T		A	L	O	U		O	T	R	A
A	R	O	M	A		H	E	E	L		L	O	O	P

45

B	R	E	D		F	O	S	S	E		F	L	I	T
R	O	T	E		A	L	I	N	E		L	O	D	I
A	T	O	I		L	E	G	A	L		A	L	E	E
G	A	N	G	P	L	A	N	K		O	G	L	E	D
			N	E	O	N		E	A	R	S			
O	L	D		N	U	D	E		N	E	T	T	E	D
T	E	A	M	S	T	E	R		A	G	O	R	A	E
T	A	R	E		R	O	M		N	O	S	E		
E	V	I	N	C	E		D	I	S	S	E	V	E	R
R	E	N	D	E	R		E	S	A	U		E	D	E
			A	L	G	A		N	I	C	E			
E	L	E	C	T		F	O	O	L	H	A	R	D	Y
D	E	L	I		T	O	R	M	E		G	O	Y	A
A	M	A	T		H	O	N	E	R		E	D	E	R
M	A	N	Y		I	T	E	R	S		R	E	D	D

46

A	R	B	O	R		S	N	A	G		I	G	O	R
T	E	R	R	A		H	E	B	E		N	O	V	A
I	N	N	E	S		O	W	E	N		S	U	I	T
C	O	O	L	H	E	A	D	E	D		O	R	N	E
			E	L	L	E		E	L	U	D	E	D	
D	E	M	U	R	S		A	F	R	I	C			
A	N	O	N		I	O	L	A		N	I	C	H	E
D	I	L	A	T	E	D		S	P	E	A	R	E	R
A	D	A	G	E		E	S	T	E		N	E	A	R
			I	N	E	R	T		A	S	T	E	R	S
C	A	R	T	O	N		E	S	C	E				
A	P	I	A		N	O	N	C	H	A	L	A	N	T
P	U	N	T		E	R	G	O		D	O	G	I	E
E	R	S	E		A	D	E	N		O	C	A	L	A
R	E	E	D		D	O	L	E		G	O	R	E	S

47

C	A	I	N		B	A	C	H	S		N	A	R	A
E	L	K	E		A	L	L	O	T		A	B	E	L
L	I	E	S		L	O	O	S	E		Z	E	A	L
L	A	S	T	S	U	P	P	E	R		A	L	D	O
			E	E	S		S	A	N		R	E	E	F
M	A	N	D	A	T	E		S	E	R	E			
A	C	E		L	E	N	S		U	N	I	T	E	
T	H	E	G	A	R	D	E	N	O	F	E	D	E	N
	U	N	I	T	E		D	I						
S	E	D	A	N		C	A	L	F		E	A	T	
			M	E	T	E		E	D	I	T	O	R	S
B	A	T	A		I	L	S		M	A	E			
A	R	A	L		A	D	A	M	A	N	D	E	V	E
I	G	N	I		R	E	M	A	N		E	R	A	S
L	U	K	E		A	S	O	R	S		U	N	I	T
S	E	A	L		S	T	A	K	E		M	E	N	E

48

S	T	A	T		S	E	R	A	C		P	O	P	S
A	R	G	O		A	L	I	B	I		E	L	I	A
Y	O	U	N	E	V	E	R	C	A	N	T	E	L	L
S	T	E	E	R	A	G	E		E	A	G	L	E	
			A	N	Y		G	A	E	L				
M	O	D	E	S	T		B	A	R	D		D	E	M
I	B	I	S		C	A	B	A	L		O	R	E	
T	O	O	T	R	U	E	T	O	B	E	G	O	O	D
T	E	N		E	N	D	O	R		E	R	D	A	
S	S	E		L	I	E	N		D	A	M	S	E	L
			M	E	T	S		D	A	U				
T	W	E	E	N		B	I	R	T	H	D	A	Y	
H	E	A	R	T	B	R	E	A	K	H	O	U	S	E
E	A	R	L		L	I	A	N	E		A	N	T	A
E	R	N	E		T	A	T	A	R		R	E	A	R

49

H	A	R	P		A	B	A	C	A		A	P	O	D
E	C	H	O		C	A	R	A	T		M	I	M	E
W	H	I	M		R	H	Y	T	H	M	I	C	A	L
S	E	N	A	T	E	S		L	U	S	T	R	E	
			O	D	E	S		R	E	E	D	S		
A	R	C	E	D		C	H	A	T		I	R	M	A
C	H	E	S	S		R	U	S	E		S	H	O	P
T	O	R		S	E	M	I	S		I	N	A		
O	D	O	R		T	O	B	E		A	S	N	E	R
R	A	S	E		A	L	A	R		R	H	E	T	T
			L	I	N	E	S		D	E	U	S		
E	R	R	A	N	D		S	E	A	T	T	L	E	
R	H	A	P	S	O	D	Y	I	N		T	O	U	R
R	E	F	S		F	E	E	L	S		E	N	N	A
S	A	T	E		F	L	A	K	E		R	E	A	L

50

A	J	A	R		S	T	A	R	S		A	H	A	B
S	O	S	O		P	E	L	E	E		N	A	N	A
T	H	E	B	I	L	L	O	F	R	I	G	H	T	S
A	N	A		D	I	E	T		G	R	E	A	S	E
			S	O	N	G		B	E	A	R			
H	A	T	T	I	E		E	L	A	N		S	L	O
A	C	R	I	D		I	N	O	N		S	H	O	W
T	H	E	C	O	N	S	T	I	T	U	T	I	O	N
L	E	E	K		O	L	E	S		N	U	R	S	E
O	D	D		A	V	E	R		B	I	C	K	E	R
			F	R	E	T		M	A	C	K			
A	L	A	R	U	M		C	U	B	E		W	H	O
D	E	C	E	M	B	E	R	F	I	F	T	E	E	N
D	A	L	E		E	L	A	T	E		V	E	R	Y
S	P	U	D		R	I	G	I	D		A	P	E	X

51

C	A	G	E		L	I	S	T		G	A	L	B	A
O	R	A	L		A	S	H	E		O	L	I	O	S
N	O	L	I		W	E	A	R		S	A	M	O	A
G	O	O	D	B	Y	E	M	R	C	H	I	P	S	
A	M	P	E	R	E		E	Y	R	E				
			I	R	A		E	N	I	S	L	E		
W	A	L	E	D		B	A	G	S		T	E	A	R
A	F	A	R	E	W	E	L	L	T	O	A	R	M	S
C	A	D	I		A	L	E	E		P	L	E	A	T
O	R	D	E	A	L		E	P	I					
			E	D	G	E		A	N	O	M	I	E	
	T	H	E	G	O	O	D	B	Y	E	G	I	R	L
B	O	I	T	E		L	I	R	E		I	N	A	T
A	R	E	N	A		E	L	E	E		V	E	T	O
R	E	D	A	N		M	E	W	S		E	D	E	N

52

S	T	O	A		B	E	S	T		D	E	F	T	
T	E	A	M		D	E	N	T	O		E	T	U	I
E	L	S	A		E	N	D	O	W		Y	A	R	D
W	E	T	S	O	N	E	S	W	H	I	S	T	L	E
			S	R	I		S	E	C					
R	G	S		A	Z	O	V		E	I	F	F	E	L
E	N	T	O		E	R	I	N		A	G	O	R	A
T	O	O	T	O	N	E	S	O	W	N	H	O	R	N
E	M	P	T	Y		L	A	S	H		I	D	E	A
M	E	S	S	E	S		S	H	I	P		S	D	S
			R	A	S		M	O	S					
D	R	U	M	S	U	P	B	U	S	I	N	E	S	S
R	O	T	A		T	E	A	S	E		A	T	O	M
E	V	E	S		E	N	J	O	Y		R	O	S	E
W	E	S	T		S	T	A	S		K	N	O	W	

211

53

```
AGRA   SPCA   HALS
POILU  OLES   ESAU
HEADLINERS    AIDE
 SLANG   NOONDAY
   ANDI   REP
MUSH  OOP   TEHEE
ANCE  RIOT   DOVER
IDEA  ENTER   NERO
LENDS  GENE   ENID
RELET  NOD   STES
  IWO   TRAP
 SIGNORI   CROWD
TUSH  HEADTOHEAD
ABET  ODRA   PINTO
USES  TOYS   ODES
```

54

```
VEST  TACT   RECAP
ORTH  HEAR   AROSE
IRAE  ERMA   FORTE
CORNUCOPIA   SNAP
ELTORO   THAIS
  SUMAC   AROUSE
RICE  IBOS   ANGLE
ADO   CORNS   AOK
SERBS  UNIT   ERGS
HENRYS   YPRES
 SEDAN   EXCESS
HAHA  CORNSTARCH
EMOTE  VIES   PARA
MOCHA  ETRE   ETAL
INKER  LADD   DOME
```

55

```
SAPOR  COCA   GRAB
ARUBA  AWOL   LIMA
MAGIC  NINE   ADES
  SECONDFIDDLE
ASP  MANGE   DELIS
CLEMENS  NAE   EAT
TARO    ISLAM
 VIOLONCELLIST
  REVUE    ECHO
TIP  AID   ABELARD
AMASS  EAMON   MUD
  MARCHINGBAND
ARLO  MEAL   EIDER
LEON  ESNE   AVILA
ETRE  TSAR   DEMIT
```

56

```
GIG  ALAMO   CROOK
APR  NOMAD   HORDE
NEO  TROIS   RUDDY
ECU  HALL   TOG
FASCINE   MANHOLE
 CELL   SEN   BOX
  ELY  INA  AIRE
CHEESEANDKISSES
RANK  AGA   AMT
ERI   ROI   PEBA
EDDYING   STIRRER
  ESS   CHIN   ORE
MORAL  PRONG   KIN
EVERE  ROUGE   EEE
LOESS  OPTED   NSW
```

57

```
SHOW   LAT   SEP
HESA  CYRUS   DOOR
EXURBANITE   ONCE
 PUNXSUTAWNEY
POE  IDEE   KEENE
ENROLLS   STILTED
LEGATE   JOHN
TROT  MAUDE   VIAL
SASS   SCARCE
REDFISH   RHETORS
ENOLA   GEAR   NEE
 GROUNDHOGDAY
GAME  AUDIOMETER
APES  BELOW   GALE
ETD   SYN   GUFF
```

58

```
ATRI  PAAND   USED
SEAT  RADIO   SALE
WATEROUZEL   ANIL
ELEMIS  ECON   DDE
   NIB  EMENDED
PEDESTAL   IDEO
ALINE  BEET   GLEN
CARD  MATTE   ALIE
ANTE  ARUT   STARE
 YARN  PESTERED
PATRIOT   SAO
ARR  ALIF   CREASE
NEIL  EARTHMOVER
DACE  TRINE   KERN
ASKS  EATAT   ARTS
```

59

```
TATE FACTO DALI
ALAN LURID URAL
RARA ADORE MAME
PITCHPIPE EBBED
     TAPE SELF
ENE LEND ELOPES
COMMERCE NEURAL
LIMA EEK NORA
ARENAE DECADENT
TETHER SROS MSS
    AREA ONTO
STENO MISTAKING
LARD TOSEE INON
ECOL EVANS ETTA
DOSE TENET SOAR
```

60

```
SHAVE PRIM BONO
LACES AURA EWES
OVERTURNED ANOA
TESTATE SEATING
   ITERS ODENSE
GRACES PAVING
RITAS CADET UGH
IDOL PACER SPRY
PEN ERNES CUTUP
 ENDEAR THROBS
 SAMUEL SPOON
OVERRUN RELATES
BINS DEBASEMENT
ESTE ERAT REATA
ROSS SORE ASSET
```

61

```
PALM PTAS BREED
ALOE LECH OUTRE
RIOT ERIE PRONE
CAKESANDALE NOM
    OAS VIED
BEERBARRELPOLKA
OVA UNIE SNARL
NERD TEASE TROT
ERTES TEXT UNO
STOUTHEARTEDMEN
    SEAL RNA
SNA WITCHESBREW
CALLA OLAM BENE
AVOIR RAZE LAOS
TYPED OWES ERST
```

62

```
AMATEUR PROMOTE
RELEASE AERATES
GAGARIN PIRATES
ESES STAYS SOME
NUR ARR MIN
TRIO FLEUR DANE
SEALERS SARONGS
    DOE VAN
CASINOS PENNAME
ALAE NEARS ASAN
LAR EPI PRC
OMAN ARENA MILA
RECEIVE TOUAREG
IDEATES ENSCENE
CANTERS RECEDED
```

63

```
THANT ACHE HORA
IONIA RAID ALAD
PUTTINONTHERITZ
 REALISTS LEVEE
    SPEW CAMELS
GOTUP EDENS
IRANI TBAR KIM
BEGINTHEBEGUINE
ELS REFS ISLAM
 SPEAR DENSE
ELATES IRED
SONAR MEATIEST
SINGININTHERAIN
ERIE OLDE SMILE
NEED BOSS TALLY
```

64

```
ETAS SAKE LASER
LASH PROW APPLE
YMCA ACRE REALM
SPARETHEROD REI
 APEX ASP CENT
    PAR SPUR
RESTRAINT ERICA
IMPRESCRIPTIBLE
PRAYS HALITOSIS
 ROSH LEI
APEN OPT SLUE
TET SPARECHANGE
LAINE SODA SIGN
ARROW SUES ATON
SLEDS ETNA LENA
```

65

```
A B C S   G A O L     S G T
R O R Y   A T R I A   A T L I
G R A N D S T A N D   N O U N
O U T G O   A N N E   A N G E
      E R R   G E N T L E
F I B   M O T E T   R O W S
A N I   L A S   L E G A T E
C A R A V E L   H A S S L E D
E N D U E S   P E R   L E G
E D D A   C I R C A   S L Y
  O I L E R S   H E M
S A G T   M E T A   R A C E S
I N G E   M O O N L I G H T S
L I E D   A L L O Y   M O A T
O L D     E S N E   A W L S
```

66

```
T O P I C   A T W A R   R A M
A B U R R   T H E M E   O T O
P I G E O N H O L E D   U S N
E E S   W O E   D R A G N E T
      A B O R T   I N A D A Y
H I T M A N   H E C T O R
O N A I R   M E T A   L O C K
P A L   S H E B A N G   B O N
I N K S   O R E L   O F I C E
  T H A M E S   F O R N O W
S Q U I R E   T O R S O
P U R P O S E   Z E E   A B E
A O K   S P R E A D E A G L E
R T E   E U L E R   G R E E N
K A Y   A N E C K   G I D D Y
```

67

```
  B A L L   E S C E   S P A T
M A R I E   N E A R   P A L E
A T S E A   C A L I   E C O N
G O O F F H A L F C O C K E D
I N N   B A M   C I A
    J U M P E D T H E G U N
P A C E D   P E A S   I R E
A R A B   A P H I D   A N G E
C A M   I D E A   U N G E R
T R I G G E R H A P P Y
    S E E   L O S   S P A
S H O O T F R O M T H E H I P
W I L D   L I M O   O R A L E
A L E E   A L A S   T I M E D
B O S S   P E R T   S E E D
```

68

```
C E N T S   S T I R   B R I M
A L E U T   H A N A   R O S E
L O R N A D O O N E   A T O M
L I E   N E W     A G A T E
A S I A   L U C Y A S H T O N
S E D G E   P R A M S   O P T
A Y S   O K A   R E O
    B R E T T A S H L E Y
S P A   R E T   L A G
P A R   M I N I S   R O V E D
A L I C E A D A M S   S O M A
T A T A R   O L E   L E M
I N O N   B E C K Y S H A R P
A C N E   E L S E   T I N G E
L E E S   E Y A S   E N T E R
```

69

```
B R O W S   C R A T   A B L E
L E M O N   H E R O   P O O L
A D O R E   E T A L   B O C A
B O O K L E A R N E D   K A T
      L A T E   D A P P L E
E M B O S S   A T O N A L
L O O N   E S T E   T R A D E
B R O C A D E   S P E C T E R
A S K E D   A S T A   E E L S
  D I L A T E   T I L S I T
S C E N I C   A S I N
A H A   B O O K H O L D E R S
G I L A   R E A R   A R N E E
E V E N   N I L E   W A T E R
S E R A   S L E W   S W E D E
```

70

```
R A D S   A B B R   I C B M S
E M I T   M A L E   N O R I A
L I A R   P R O C E S S I N G
I N L A W   N O S E I N T O
C O M P A C T D I S C
      F R A I L   T A C I T
C A S S E T T E     M O R E
I M M E R S E   S E C U L A R
T O U R   R E C O R D E R
E R G O T   Y O U R S
      R E V O L U T I O N S
T H E G O L E M   A W F U L
M O D U L A T I O N   A T R A
A N N A L   T E L E   L E S T
N E A R S   E R A T   K N E E
```

214

71

S	C	A	T			S	P	O	T			M	I	M	E
H	O	H	U	M		L	E	N	A			A	R	I	L
A	D	O	R	E		O	L	E	S			Y	E	T	I
M	A	Y	F	L	O	W	E	R	S		O	N	E	A	
			E	L	S	E			E	R	N	E	S		
C	A	R	M	E	L			A	L	A	N				
A	P	I	A		A	P	E	X		S	A	I	N	T	
P	E	P	Y	S		L	E	E		H	I	T	O	R	
A	D	E	P	T		A	L	D	A		S	E	S	O	
			O	L	A	N		D	E	E	M	E	D		
	C	O	L	O	R			I	S	A	R				
M	A	C	E		M	O	N	T	H	O	F	M	A	Y	
A	R	A	D		O	R	N	E		D	R	O	S	S	
S	A	L	A		R	E	E	L		E	E	R	I	E	
S	T	A	Y		Y	O	R	E			T	E	A	R	

72

F	L	O	P			A	G	A	M	A			M	A	T	S
L	O	K	I			D	L	V	I	I			E	X	A	M
A	C	R	E			J	O	I	N	T			S	L	O	E
W	H	A	T	F	O	O	D	S		T	H	E	S	E	
			A	R	U	M			K	A	I				
S	A	P		U	R	I			S	P	A	C	E	R	
P	R	A	L	I	N	E	S		A	S	M	A	R	A	
L	A	C	E	T		R	I	B		Y	A	R	N	S	
A	D	E	S	T	E		P	E	A	C	H	P	I	E	
T	A	R	T	A	R			A	M	A		S	E	D	
			R	N	A			T	A	K	E				
A	D	M	I	T		M	O	R	S	E	L	S	B	E	
D	E	A	R		P	A	R	I	S		I	C	O	N	
Z	E	R	O		O	N	I	C	E		Z	O	R	I	
E	D	E	N		P	A	N	E	D		A	W	E	D	

73

W	H	I	F	F			S	C	A	R			P	I	E	S
E	A	S	E	L			E	R	S	E			O	R	C	A
A	R	A	R	A			C	I	N	Q			L	A	R	K
R	E	S	T	U	P		B	O	U	T	I	Q	U	E	
			I	N	R	I			T	I	N	T			
R	E	A	L	T	O	R	S		S	T	I	L	E	S	
E	L	L	E		P	A	T	R	I		C	I	N	E	
A	L	O		O	N	E	A	T			C	A	D		
L	I	S	P		S	I	N	A	I		R	I	T	E	
M	E	S	A	B	I		O	D	O	M	E	T	E	R	
			R	A	T	S			S	N	A	P			
P	R	E	T	T	I	E	R		S	T	R	I	D	E	
L	O	R	N		O	P	E	N		T	O	L	E	T	
O	P	I	E		N	I	N	E		E	V	E	N	T	
D	E	E	R		S	A	D	E		R	E	D	Y	E	

74

A	L	A	N			C	O	W			T	G	I	F
L	I	M	E		S	O	N	A	R		I	R	M	A
A	L	E	S		P	R	I	C	E		P	A	A	R
S	I	X	T	E	E	N	T	O	N	S		N	N	E
			L	A	C			D	A	M	N			
P	R	E	C	I	S			E	S	S	A	Y	S	
C	I	O		H	E	L	I	X		H	I	K	E	S
A	N	D	S		S	O	L	I	D		S	N	A	P
R	E	S	E	W		E	L	L	I	S		O	R	A
	S	T	E	A	L	S		E	V	E	N	T	S	
			E	S	S	O			I	N	A			
S	R	I		H	U	N	T	A	N	D	P	E	C	K
L	O	G	O		S	U	R	G	E		K	A	L	E
A	P	E	D		E	D	I	T	S		I	V	A	N
W	E	R	E			E	M	S			N	E	W	T

75

	F	I	B	E	R			A	P	A	C	E	
M	A	N	A	T	E	E		A	B	A	L	O	N	E
A	N	A	D	E	M	S		G	A	R	A	N	D	S
D	A	N			T	R	E			C	O	T		
A	T	I		A	C	H	E	N	E	S		E	R	E
M	I	T		T	H	E	A	T	R	E		I	S	R
	C	Y	P	H	E	R		S	E	N	A	T	E	
			E	W	E			C	D	S				
	C	A	R	A	T	S		S	T	E	A	L	S	
T	A	G		R	A	T	T	L	E	R		U	P	S
O	V	I		T	H	R	E	A	D	S		G	O	A
S	O	T			E	A	T			G	U	T		
C	R	A	S	H	E	S		E	M	A	N	A	T	E
A	T	T	A	I	N	S		D	A	M	A	G	E	D
	S	E	W	E	D			R	A	G	E	D		

76

H	A	H	A			B	R	I	C		S	L	E	W
I	C	O	S	I		R	E	N	O		H	I	D	E
S	T	R	I	N	G	E	N	C	Y		O	M	I	T
	I	N	S	T	E	A	D				E	A	T	S
			R	N	S			G	A	S				
P	U	T	S	O	U	T		S	A	R	T	R	E	
I	S	I	T			T	A	M	A	R	I	N	S	
P	H	A	R	M	A	C	O	L	O	G	I	C	A	L
S	E	R	I	A	T	I	M		N	I	T	A		
R	A	N	G	E	D		D	R	A	G	N	E	T	
			G	I	N			I	A	N				
D	E	F	T			E	S	P	O	U	S	E		
A	V	E	R		H	I	G	H	S	T	R	U	N	G
D	E	L	I		U	R	G	E		E	A	R	T	H
A	R	L	O		M	E	S	S			L	E	O	I

215

77

D	A	T	A		S	C	A	T		A	B	A	S	E
A	B	E	T		A	L	S	O		E	R	R	O	R
S	L	A	T		R	A	I	N		N	A	I	L	S
H	E	M	I	N	G	W	A	Y		E	D	D	I	E
			R	O	E	S			G	A	B			
T	A	P	E	D			P	R	E	S	U	M	E	D
I	D	A		S	T	O	L	E	N			R	O	L	E
G	O	L	F		A	N	E	A	R		Y	U	L	E
E	R	M	A		S	C	A	L	E	S		S	A	D
R	E	S	U	L	T	E	D			P	R	E	S	S
			L	I	E			T	R	I	O			
S	P	I	K	E		S	T	E	I	N	B	E	C	K
A	L	O	N	G		T	A	R	P		O	M	E	N
R	A	N	E	E		E	L	S	E		T	I	R	E
K	N	A	R	S		P	E	E	N		S	T	E	W

78

S	A	L	T	I	N	E		R	A	V	A	G	E	S
E	L	E	A	N	O	R		A	D	A	M	A	N	T
R	E	G	R	E	T	S		R	I	N	A	L	D	O
G	R	A	Z	E	R		R	E	T	E		L	O	P
E	T	T	A		E	N	A			T	A	R	P	
S	E	E	N		A	C	I	S		A	N	S	E	
	R	E	S	T		P	E	R	O	R	A	T	E	D
			A	S	P	H	A	L	T					
A	P	P	O	R	T	I	O	N		S	P	A	D	
T	R	E	Y		S	E	R	I		A	C	E	D	
T	E	L	L			S	S	S		R	E	M	I	
E	P	I		R	O	U	E		P	A	T	T	O	N
S	A	C	H	E	M	S		S	A	T	I	A	T	E
T	R	A	I	N	E	E		T	R	E	A	T	E	R
S	E	N	S	O	R	S		U	S	E	L	E	S	S

79

W	A	S	P		T	A	C	O	S		L	A	S	T
A	L	T	A		A	D	O	R	E		A	L	T	O
R	O	U	N	D	R	O	B	I	N		Z	E	A	L
D	E	N	S	E			B	O	N	E	Y	A	R	D
			Y	A	R	D		L	A	G	S			
A	S	P		L	O	O	S	E		G	U	S	T	S
C	L	U	B	S	O	D	A		A	S	S	E	R	T
H	A	L	L		F	O	L	I	O		A	R	I	A
E	N	S	U	E	S		S	T	R	A	N	G	E	R
S	T	E	E	D		F	A	C	T	S		E	S	T
			J	A	V	A		H	A	S	P			
T	E	L	E	M	A	R	K		A	L	I	G	N	
A	R	E	A		P	R	I	M	A	D	O	N	N	A
F	I	N	N		O	A	T	E	R		W	R	A	P
T	E	S	S		R	H	E	T	T		S	E	W	S

80

W	A	R	T		A	S	P	U	R		S	T	O	P
I	T	E	R		M	O	U	S	E		P	I	P	E
S	O	D	A		O	U	T	O	F	O	R	D	E	R
P	R	O	F	F	E	R	S			N	I	E	C	E
			F	I	B	S		B	I	T	T			
A	T	T	I	L	A		C	A	S	H	E	S	I	N
M	E	R	C	I		A	N	T	E			E	N	O
I	N	A		B	O	A	R	D	O	F		L	E	I
N	O	D		U	N	I	T			L	I	M	P	S
D	R	E	S	S	E	R	S		D	O	N	A	T	E
			E	T	R	E		I	R	O	N			
F	E	N	C	E		A	B	O	R	A	L	L	Y	
O	V	E	R	R	I	D	D	E	N		R	A	V	I
S	I	R	E		S	N	A	R	E		D	R	I	P
S	L	O	T		M	A	R	T	S		S	K	I	S

81

S	P	A	R		S	T	A	C	K		A	H	E	M
E	A	V	E		T	A	B	L	E		N	O	P	E
W	R	E	N		A	L	I	E	N		T	R	I	S
S	T	R	A	W	B	E	R	R	Y	F	I	N	C	H
			M	E	L			G	A	L				
B	L	U	E	B	E	R	R	Y		E	A	R	E	D
E	O	N		M	I	A		R	E	T	I	N	A	
A	I	D	E		A	O	R	T	A		A	S	T	I
C	R	E	T	I	N		E	R	I			E	E	L
H	E	R	O	D		C	R	A	N	B	E	R	R	Y
			O	P	A			D	O	N				
H	U	C	K	L	E	B	E	R	R	Y	F	I	N	N
I	R	A	N		R	A	T	I	O		A	G	I	O
S	A	N	E		C	L	A	M	P		C	O	P	S
S	L	E	W		H	A	L	E	S		E	R	S	E

82

P	A	T	S		S	L	A	M		S	T	R	I	P
O	R	A	L		P	O	L	O		I	R	A	T	E
P	E	R	E		R	E	D	O		T	A	C	I	T
	D	A	D	D	Y	W	A	R	B	U	C	K	S	
				A	L	E			A	P	T			
R	O	M	A	N	Y		E	L	M	S		C	A	N
E	R	E	C	T		A	T	U	B		S	O	T	O
F	A	T	H	E	R	C	H	R	I	S	T	M	A	S
E	T	R	E		A	M	O	K		T	A	B	L	E
R	E	O		O	N	E	S		H	A	R	O	L	D
			A	R	C			S	O	N				
	P	A	P	A	H	E	M	I	N	G	W	A	Y	
C	U	M	I	N		M	A	R	E		A	T	O	P
A	M	O	N	G		I	C	E	S		C	O	R	E
B	A	R	G	E		T	E	S	T		O	M	E	N

83

```
A C T I   B I B B S   S T A R
P R O M   U B O A T   T A L E
R A S P   S L A T E   E L M S
  T H E C H E S H I R E C A T
      D A Y       N O R
A S P E N   F I B   N I L E
C A R   A R I S E S   N A M E
C H A R L E S L D O D G S O N
T I T O   S T E E L E   E T O
B E A N   S S W   N A R E S
      D T H       R E B
T H E W H I T E R A B B I T
R A T A   R E D A N   O D E S
A R T Y   E L E C T   T E N S
P I E S   D E N E S   S A T E
```

84

```
  A R C S   F O B S   T A D
C L O U T   J E E P   V E N I
H O B B Y H O R S E   E D N A
E N E   M A R   S C A N D A L
R E S C I N D S   T R O Y
      P E G   P R E A M B L E
P A P A S   H A I R     E O N
I R I S   B A N N S   M A I D
L E G   A R I D   E A R N S
L A G G A R D S   A N I
  Y U R T   H A L F M A S T
A R B I T E R   T O O   B E A
D E A D   R U B B E R D U C K
Z A N E   E L I A   C A S T E
E L K   D E N T   E W E S
```

85

```
C A L M   B O M B S   C E N T
A L O E   A D U L T   O D O R
D E R N   R A D I O   R E N O
R U D D E R     G R I N N E D
E T H E R   S C H E M E
    A L R I G H T   P A B L O
L O W   B T U   A S L E E P
A S H   O S C A R     L I T
P E A R L S   K S U   L D S
P E W E E   P L E N A R Y
      P O S I E S   C O L O R
S M I L I N G     S E N A T E
H O R A   A L I C E   D U E L
U P O N   G E N I E   O G R E
T E N T   S T E E R   S H O T
```

86

```
M A L T   E R R O R   H A S P
A S O R   G O O S E   A L T O
S T R I N G B E A N   M E A T
S A D N E S S   K I S S E R S
      E T H   M A N E T
E T A   S E T A     T R A M
V E R B   L E E R   T I D A L
A M P O U L E   I R O N A G E
S P A W N   M A T E   G R I N
  O S S A   S A L T   E C T
    T R E E S   A R U
D O O R M A T   S P O N D E E
R A N I   S H O E S T R I N G
A H E N   E E R I E   I N T O
B U R G   S L E D S   G E E S
```

87

```
S C A R   L I A R S   A C I D
A O N E   A N N I E   S O D A
P R O T E C T I O N   K N E W
S E N O R   O T T   B I S O N
      R I P   A S C E N T
L E C T E R N   O R G A N
A L O E   O I L I N G   B O W
S E N D   P L O D S   S L O E
T N T   F E E B L E   P E N N
  A R I E L   E N C A S E D
    A B U S E D   T A R
E B B E D   G I A   D R O O P
R O A R   P R O P R I E T O R
M I N I   M E D E A   R O N A
A L D A   S T E R N   S E A M
```

88

```
A P I S   A R M S   T O A S T
L O R E   B A I T   O N C U E
A P E X   E M M A   S O R E L
M I N T S   B I R D S   O D E
O N E O C L O C K J U M P
    N R A     S P O O L S
A L I   E S T E S   S L I T
S O M E W H E R E I N T I M E
P O P E   D A C C A   S A W
S P A R T A     E N D
  R O U N D M I D N I G H T
B E T   R A R E R   Y A H O O
A L I E N   A L A S   L A M P
S L A T E   M O N A   O N E S
S A L A D   A N I L   G A R Y
```

89

G	N	A	W		S	C	R	A	P		S	P	E	W
I	A	G	O		P	O	I	S	E		L	E	V	I
S	T	A	R	S	A	N	D	S	T	R	I	P	E	S
H	O	I	S	T		V	E	T		A	M	P	L	E
		N	E	A	T	E	R		F	R	E	E		
B	U	S		I	C	Y		D	I	E		R	E	D
A	T	T	E	N	U	A	T	E	D		O	M	A	R
K	I	T	T	S		B	A	M		D	R	I	V	E
E	C	H	O		A	L	L	O	P	H	O	N	E	S
R	A	E		R	Y	E		N	E	A		T	D	S
		G	M	E	N		R	I	P	R	A	P		
A	T	R	E	E		T	I	A		M	E	A	T	S
C	H	A	R	L	I	E	M	C	C	A	R	T	H	Y
C	O	I	L		D	R	E	A	D		I	T	E	M
T	U	N	E		S	I	D	L	E		E	Y	E	S

90

A	L	A	M	P		D	I	S	H		I	D	O	L
J	A	M	I	E		A	N	T	E		R	E	M	O
A	K	I	S	S		D	I	A	L		A	M	E	N
R	E	D	S	K	Y	A	T	M	O	R	N	I	N	G
			E	Y	E			P	T	A				
G	A	L	S		M	O	P	S		C	A	R	E	D
A	R	A		E	R	A			E	M	I	L	Y	
M	O	R	N	I	N	G	S	A	T	S	E	V	E	N
	A	M	A	T	I		M	E	E	K		O	R	E	S
S	P	A				Y	A	P						
H	O	W	I	H	A	T	E	T	O	G	E	T	U	P
E	V	E	R		R	U	S	E		I	N	A	N	E
R	A	R	E		E	R	S	E		L	E	N	I	N
B	L	E	D		S	E	E	M		E	D	G	E	S

91

O	D	I	N		W	E	B	S		A	L	O	F	T
L	A	M	E		A	L	O	E		R	I	L	E	D
E	M	P	H	A	S	I	Z	E		T	E	A	M	S
G	E	O	R	G	I	A	O	K	E	E	F	F	E	
		R	U	E				S	E	R				
D	I	T		S	A	W	S		K	I	S	M	E	T
A	R	A	S		R	O	T	S		A	L	I	B	I
K	E	N	T	U	C	K	Y	C	O	L	O	N	E	L
A	N	C	O	N		S	L	A	B		P	E	R	T
R	E	E	L	E	D		E	R	I	C		S	T	S
			N	O	G				O	A	T			
	R	H	O	D	E	I	S	L	A	N	D	R	E	D
N	A	O	M	I		B	L	A	C	K	H	O	L	E
A	S	P	E	N		B	O	R	E		O	N	A	N
T	H	I	N	G		S	E	A	S		C	E	N	T

92

S	O	L	D		S	T	A	R		A	S	T	O	
A	L	O	E		H	E	R	B	S		B	U	R	L
L	A	M	B		O	P	T	I	C		E	G	A	D
A	F	B		T	R	E	Y		A	F	L	A	M	E
		A	R	E	T	E		B	R	I	E	R		
S	T	R	O	L	L		B	E	L	T		M	A	C
A	U	D	I	L	E		R	E	E		B	A	L	L
I	D	Y	L		A	P	O	R	T		U	P	T	O
L	O	P	S		F	E	W		O	U	T	L	A	W
S	R	O		S	P	A	N		A	S	T	E	R	N
		P	E	T	I	T		S	K	E	E	T		
G	O	L	D	E	N		A	C	T	S		R	T	E
A	L	A	I		E	N	T	E	R		N	E	A	R
S	E	R	F		S	E	I	N	E		R	E	D	S
P	O	S	Y		E	P	E	E		A	S	S	T	

93

C	A	R	T		A	S	S	E	T		S	L	O	T
H	I	E	R		R	E	A	C	H		P	E	T	E
E	D	D	I	E	M	A	P	L	E		R	A	T	A
R	E	S	A	L	E		S	A	O		U	S	E	R
			L	I	R	A		T	R	A	C	E	R	Y
A	O	K		A	S	P	S		E	R	E			
C	L	A	P	S		P	A	L	M	I	S	T	R	Y
H	A	L	O		E	L	V	I	S		U	R	I	S
E	V	E	R	G	R	E	E	N		A	P	A	C	E
			C	I	O		D	E	R	N		P	E	R
I	M	P	U	L	S	E		R	E	T	E			
L	O	O	P		I	L	E		M	I	S	L	E	D
L	I	L	I		O	L	D	H	I	C	K	O	R	Y
A	R	A	N		N	I	N	E	S		E	G	A	N
T	A	R	E		S	E	A	R	S		R	O	S	E

94

G	A	B	O	R		S	C	A	M		C	R	E	E
A	B	O	V	E		H	A	L	O		H	A	L	L
F	L	E	E	T		A	C	E	D		A	B	U	M
F	E	R	R	I	S	W	H	E	E	L	R	I	D	E
			R	O	L	E		R	U	D	D	E	R	
H	A	S	T	E	N				A	N	N			
A	L	T	O		A	L	E	C		G	A	S	E	S
T	O	A	F	A	R	E	T	H	E	E	W	E	L	L
S	T	R	U	M		C	A	E	N		N	A	S	A
			O	O	H				D	I	S	N	E	Y
A	T	H	A	N	D		L	O	O	M				
C	H	A	R	G	E	D	A	F	F	A	I	R	E	S
R	O	S	S		S	U	R	F		G	R	O	V	E
I	S	T	O		S	A	V	E		E	M	B	E	R
D	E	A	N		A	L	A	R		S	A	B	R	E

95

```
WAGS CLAM   BAAL
ELAM ROXY  SALSA
LOPE ADIT  KNOTS
SHELLFISH  IDEAS
HARLOT   SETS
    TYRO ASHCAN
STABS UMPS  ERIE
IAGO FLEET  LEDA
ARAM LEGS  CLEAR
MARBLE ATTU
   SODA  ARAFAT
OMAHA SHELLGAME
BORED TOLE  ATAR
EVILS OMAN  TASS
YELL RENT   ELSE
```

96

```
ALMA GRACE  BATH
FOAM AIDES  OGRE
ACRE GLASS  BEER
ROYROGERS  THREE
    IVES  AGRO
SPACED   TEAPOT
LOGAN THIN  EPIC
ALA SERIOUS  ILA
GLIB DAMN  TUNER
SNORED   PAPERS
   DINE  KAID
ACTED SANDRADEE
DOOR EMBER  TILL
ANNE GABLE  EVAS
MEEK GNATS  DANE
```

97

```
BOSS RADAR  ALAN
ABUT EVADE  COLE
SOFA VOTEGETTER
HEFT EWE  RAISED
   REARS  BES
FEASTS BUTTRESS
ERG EAMES  SALTY
VOID LEASE  JEAN
EDSEL ARENA  CRO
RETRACTS DIETED
   NAY  SOLDO
APPEAL SIR  IRAN
CANDIDATES TALE
ERIN ELITE  OTOE
DANA RARER  REED
```

98

```
SPIN PAYER  OAST
HINT ALIVE  UTAH
ONTHEROPES TOFU
WOE ROGER  OOZED
STRAND   STIFF
   TEY  CABLES
COILS TAKE  OUST
ANNO LACES  URSA
NERO OXEN  SNEER
TIESUP   ETD
   ENSUE LASSOS
AGREE SMEAR  OUI
MIEN HAMSTRINGS
AVID AGATE  RAHS
HENS YESES  ARTY
```

99

```
ADIEU ANA  QUASH
LANAS BER  UNITE
GISTS OHM  IDLES
ESTER ARA  TREES
RYAN GRUMP  EYRE
   LURED  EATS
YELPER INGESTED
ERE SMATTER  HOI
ANDBEANS ASPENS
   ETNA  ONEIN
ASST EGYPT  CERA
STERE RAT  STEAM
CODAS ALI  NUDGE
OKAYS MIO  ARLES
TENSE SEN  PEERS
```

100

```
PAST PRUNE  CPAS
ALTI ACRID  ORCA
PIER RANTS  LENS
ABRADE   REPOSES
WINNINGCOLORS
   ANTAL  SAGA
CAD GALEN  DALE
THECOLOROFMONEY
SOSO PILEA  GEE
   TELE  CLANG
COLORSERGEANT
NARRATE   LONGER
OLAF HAGUE  DARE
SITU EDITS  ENVY
HEEL RENES  RAYS
```